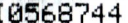

SWU-NAP- 013

UNIFORMS OF RUSSIAN ARMY DURING THE NAPOLEONIC WAR VOL.8

UNDER THE REIGN OF ALEXANDER I
EMPEROR OF RUSSIA BETWEEN 1801 AND 1825
ARMY INFANTRY: GRENADIER'S REGIMENTS

From the Viskovatov's greatest work:
"Historical description of the clothing and
arms of the Russian Army"

English translation by Mark Conrad

SOLDIERSHOP PUBLISHING

AUTHOR

Aleksandr Vasilevich Viskovatov born 22 April (4 May New Style) 1804, died 27 February (11 March) 1858 in St. Petersburg, Russian military historian. He graduated from the 1st Cadet Corps and served in the artillery, the hydrographic depot of the Naval Ministry, and then in the Department of Military Educational Institutions. He mainly studied historical artifacts and the histories of military units. Viskovatov's greatest work was the Historical Description of the Clothing and Arms of the Russian Army.

TRANSLATOR

Mark Conrad is an American historian with a great interest for all the Russian history.

Title: **UNIFORMS OF RUSSIAN ARMY DURING THE NAPOLEONIC WAR VOL. 8 -**
Army Infantry: Grenadier's regiments 1801-1825
By A.V.Viskovatov. English translation by Mark Conrad. First edition by Soldiershop.
Cover & Art Design: Luca S. Cristini. Plates re-colorations by Anna Cristini
ISBN code: 978-88-93270991

Published by Soldiershop publishing, via Padre Davide, 7 - 24050 Zanica (BG) ITALY. www.soldiershop.com

UNIFORMS
OF THE RUSSIAN
ARMY DURING THE
NAPOLEONIC WAR VOL.8

UNDER THE REIGN OF ALEXANDER I EMPEROR OF
RUSSIA BETWEEN 1801 AND 1825

*

Army infantry: Grenadier's regiments

Alexander I (1802 c.) by Stepan Shchukin

HISTORICAL DESCRIPTION OF THE CLOTHING AND ARMS OF THE RUSSIAN ARMY - A.V. VISKOVATOV

(First English translation by Mark Conrad)

Soldiershop is glad to presents the complete collection of the great job made by A.V. Viskovatov dedicated to the uniforms and weapons belonging to the Russian army during the Napoleonic period, until 1825. The time we considered corresponds to the reigns of two Tzars: Paul I, who reigned since 1769 until his murder on the 23rd of March 1801, and his son Aleksandr Pavlovi☐ Romanov, that with the title of Alexander I, sat on the throne until the 1st December 1825.

Our reprint in based on the original 19th century volumes, to be precise the volumes from 7 to 9 are dedicated to the reign of Paul I; this first part is distributed on 7 volumes, having a numbering from 1 to 7. From number 10 to 18 of the original volumes, the second part is dedicated to the Russian troops under Alexander I. These still being worked on and they will be soon ready, distributed on twenty volumes approximately. Our new edition, the first ever published in English, both on paper and digital format, boasts a large number of color plates, many of them unpublished and coloured by our team of expert artists and scholars of uniformology. Each volume is based on 50/70 plates, always accompanied by the original translated text which describes the uniforms, the organization and the armament of the Russian army of the period.

A unique work in its genre, a must have in any respecting collection!
Aleksandr Vasilevich Viskovatov born 22 April (4 May New Style) 1804, died 27 February (11 March) 1858 in St. Petersburg, Russian military historian. He graduated from the 1st Cadet Corps and served in the artillery, the hydrographic depot of the Naval Ministry, and then in the Department of Military Educational Institutions.

He mainly studied historical artifacts and the histories of military units. Viskovatov's greatest work was the Historical Description of the Clothing and Arms of the Russian Army (Vols. 1-30, St. Petersburg, 1841-62; 2nd ed. Vols. 1-34, St. Petersburg - Novosibirsk - Leningrad, 1899-1948). This work is based on a great quantity of archival documents and contains four thousand colored illustrations.

Viskovatov was the author of Chronicles of the Russian Army (Books 1-20, St. Petersburg, 1834-42) and Chronicles of the Russian Imperial Army (Parts 1-7, St. Petersburg, 1852). He collected valuable material on the history of the Russian navy which went into A Short Overview of Russian Naval Campaigns and General Voyages to the End of the XVII Century (St. Petersburg, 1864; 2nd edition Moscow, 1946). Together with A.I. Mikhailovskii-Danilevskii he helped prepare and create the Military Gallery in the Winter Palace.

He wrote the historical military inscriptions for the walls of the Hall of St. George in the Great Palace of the Kremlin. (From the article in the Soviet Military Encyclopedia.)

CONTENTS

*

RUSSIAN ARMY,
Organization 1801-1825 1st part

CHANGES IN THE COMPOSITION AND NOMENCLATURE OF ALL FORCES, FROM 1801 TO 1825

Military Land Forces on 12 March, 1801 - I.   Army Infantry.

On the day of Alexander I's ascension to the Throne, 12 March, 1801, the Military Land forces of the Russian Empire consisted of the following troops:

I.) Guards Infantry: Leib-Gvardii EGO IMPERATORSKAGO VELICHESTVA polk [Life-Guards HIS IMPERIAL MAJESTY'S Regiment] (formerly the Preobrazhenskii) – of four (five-company) Grenadier battalions and two flank companies [fligel-roty]; Leib-Gv. Ego Imperatorskago Vysochestva Aleksandra Pavlovicha polk [Life-Gds. His Imperial Highness Alexander Pavlovich's Regiment] (formerly the Semenovskii) – of three (five-company) Grenadier battalions and one flank company; L.-Gv. Ego Imperatorskago Vysochestva Nikolaya Pavlovicha polk [L.-Gds. His Imperial Highness Nicholas Pavlovich's Regiment] (formerly the Ismailovskoe) – of three (five-company) Grenadier battalions and one flank company; Leib-Gv. Yegerskii batalion [Life-Gds. Jäger Battalion] – of four companies; and the Leib-Gvardii Garnizonnyi batalion [Life-Guards Garrison Battalion] – of three companies.

II.) Guards Cavalry: Kavalergardskii polk [Chevalier Guards Regiment] – of three squadrons; L.-Gv.Ego Imperatorskago Vysochestva Konstantina Pavlovicha polk [L.-Gds. His Imperial Highness Constantine Pavlovich's Regiment] (formerly the Leib-Gv. konnyi polk [Life-Gds. Horse Regiment]) – of five squadrons; Leib-Gvardii Gusarskii polk [Life-Guards Hussar Regiment] – of two five-squadron battalions; and the Leib-Kazachii polk [Life-Cossack Regiment] – of three squadrons.

III.) Guards Artillery: Artilleriiskii Ego Imperatorskago Vysochestva Mikhaila Pavlovicha batalion [His Imperial Highness Michael Pavlovich's Artillery Battalion] (formerly the Leib-Gvardii Artilleriiskii batalion] – of five foot companies [peshiya roty] and one horse company [konnaya rota], and three commands [komandy]: the Pionernaya, Pontonnaya, and Furshtatskaya [Pioneer, Pontoon, and Supply-Train].

IV.) Grenadier Regiments [Grenaderskie polki]: Leib [Life], Kerbitsa [Kerbits'] (formerly the Pavlovskii), Palintsyna [Palintsyn's] (formerly the Yekaterinoslavskii, later the Pskovskii), Sakena 1-go [Sacken 1st's] (formerly the S.-Peterburgskii), Naslednago Printsa Meklenburgskago [The Hereditary Prince of Mecklenburg's] (formerly the Astrakhanskii), Passeka [Passek's] (formerly the Kievskii), Printsa Karla Meklenburgskago [Prince Carl of Mecklenburg's] (formerly the Moskovskii [Moscow]), Berkha [Berg's] (formerly the Malorossiiskii [Little Russia, or Ukraine]), Bakhmeteva 3-go [Bakhmetev 3rd's] (formerly the Sibirskii [Siberia]), Mamaeva [Mamaev's] (formerly the Fanagoriiskii [Phanagoria]), Titova 1-go [Titov 1st's] (formerly the Khersonskii), Danzasa [Danzas's] (formerly the Tavricheskii [Taurica]), and Tuchkova 2-go [Tuchkov 2nd's] (formerly the Kavkazskii [Caucasus]); the first being of four Grenadier battalions and the rest of two Fusilier battalions and two Grenadier, or flank, companies, while the battalions were of five companies.

V.) Musketeer Regiments [Mushketerskie polki]: Sedmoratskago [Sedmoratskii's] (formerly the Belozerskii), Yermolova [Yermolov's] (formerly the Nasheburgskii), Essena 1-go [Essen 1st's] (formerly the Chernigovskii), Barona Rozena [Baron Rozen's] (formerly the Novoingermanlandskii [New Ingermanland]), Lasunskago 1-go [Lasunskii 1st's] (formerly the Yaroslavskii), Miloradovicha [Miloradovich's] (formerly the Apsheronskii), Repninskago [Repninskii's] (formerly the Smolenskii), Grafa Lanzherona [Graf Langeron's] (formerly the Ryazhskii), Prshibyshevskago [Prshibyshevskii's] (formerly the Kurskii), Maksheeva [Maksheev's] (formerly the Kozlovskii), Serbina [Serbin's] (formerly the Sevastopolskii), Mansurova 1-go [Mansurov 1st's] (formerly the

Belevskii), Loveiki [Loveika's] (formerly the Aleksopolskii), Izmailova [Izmailov's] (formerly the Shlisselburgskii [Schlüsselburg]), Lidersa [Lüders'] (formerly the Bryanskii), Borozdina 2-go [Borozdin 2nd's] (formerly the Troitskii), Sukina 2-go [Sukin 2nd's] (formerly the Ladozhskii [Ladoga]), Tinkova [Tinkov's] (formerly the Polotskii), Kamenskago 2-go [Kamenskii 2nd's] (formerly the Arkhangelogorodskii [Archangel]), Engelgardta [Englehardt's] (formerly the Staroingermanlandskii [Old Ingermanland]), Fertcha [Fertch's] (formerly the Novgorodskii), Khitrovo [Khitrovo's] (formerly the Nizhegorodskii [Nizhnii-Novgorod]), Musina-Pushkina [Musin-Pushkin's] (formerly the Vitebskii), Selekhova [Selekhov's] (formerly the Azovskii), Brunova [Brunov's] (formerly the Orlovskii [Orel]), Khotuntseva [Khotuntsev's] (formerly the Revelskii [Reval]), Drekselya [Drexel's] (formerly the Tulskii [Tula]), Yefimovicha [Yefimovich's] (formerly the Yeletskii), Golenishcheva-Kutuzova [Golenishchev-Kutuzov's] (formerly the Pskovskii), Fershtera [Ferster's] (formerly the Tambovskii), Mitskago [Mitskii's] (formerly the Rostovskii), Petrovskago [Petrovskii's] (formerly the Muromskii), Bykova [Bykov's] (formerly the Staroskolskii [Staryi-Oskol]), Garina [Garin's] (formerly the Tobolskii), Leonteva [Leontev's] (formerly the Tiflisskii), Arsenv'eva [Arsenev's] (formerly the Voronezhskii), Knorringa 2-go [Knorring 2nd's] (formerly the Kazanskii), Fensha [Fensh's] (formerly the Moskovskii [Moscow]), Gulyakova [Gulyakov's] (formerly the Kabardinskii [Kabarda]), Rozenberga [Rosenberg's] (formerly the Vladimirskii), Gersdorfa [Gersdorf's] (formerly the Uglitskii [Uglich]), Tuchkova 1-go [Tuchkov 1st's] (formerly the Sevskii), Rodgofa [Rothof's] (formerly the Narvskii), Konovicha [Konovich's] (formerly the Dneprovskii [Dnieper]), Manteifelya [Manteufel's] (formerly the Vyatskii [Vyatka]), Shenshina [Shenshin's] (formerly the Suzdalskii), Verderevskago [Verderevskii's] (formerly the Keksgolmskii [Kexholm]), Ganzhi 1-go [Gandzha 1st's] (formerly the Vyborgskii [Viborg]), Alekseeva [Alekseev's] (formerly the Ryazanskii), Knyazya Gorchakova 1-go [Prince Gorchakov 1st's] (formerly the Nevskii [Neva]), Kastelliya [Castellii's] (formerly the Velikolutskii [Velikie-Luki]), Nechaeva [Nechaev's] (formerly the Sofiiskii [Sofiya]), Lavrova [Lavrov's] (formerly the Shirvanskii), Rittera [Ritter's] (formerly the Permskii), Gr. Shembeka [Graf Szembek's] (formerly the Nizovskii), Malyshkina [Malyshkin's] (formerly the Butyrskii), Tsybulskago [Tsybulskii's] (formerly the Ufimskii [Ufa]), Bakhmeteva 1-go [Bakhmetev 1st's] (formerly the Rylskii), Pevtsova [Pevtsov's] (formerly the Yekaterinburgskii), Kupfershmita [Kupferschmidt's] (formerly the Selenginskii), Knyazya Vyazemskago [Prince Vyazemskii's] (formerly the Tomskii), Kn. Shcherbatova [Prince Shcherbatov's] (formerly Arkharova 1-go [Arkhorov 1st's]), Runicha 1-go [Runich 1st's] (formerly Pavlutskago [Pavlutskii's]), Kashkina [Kashkin's] (formerly Branta [Brant's]), Nesvetaeva[Nesvetaev's] (formerly Leitnera [Leitner's]), Millera 1-go [Müller 1st's] (formerly of the same name), Anikeeva [Anikeev's] (formerly Marklovskago [Marklovskii's]), Baklanovskago [Baklanovskii's] (formerly Berkha [Berg's]), and Ushakova [Ushakov's] (formerly the Senatskii [Senate]); each—of two Musketeer battalions and two Grenadier companies, with each battalion—of five companies.

VI.) Jäger Regiments [Yegerskie polki]: Mikhelsona 2-go [Michelson 2nd's] (formerly the 2nd Jäger Regiment), Gvozdeva [Gvozdev's] (formerly the 3rd), Barklaya-de-Tolli [Barclay-de-Tolly's] (formerly the 4th), Bradke [Bradke's] (formerly the 5th), Alfimova [Alfimov's] (formerly the 6th), Grafa Ivelicha 3-go [Graf Ivelich 3rd's] (formerly the 7th), Millera [Müller's] (formerly the 8th), Priudy [Priuda's] (formerly the 9th), Veidemeiera [Weidemeier's] (formerly the 10th), Markova [Markov's] (formerly the 11th), Bally [Balla's] (formerly the 12th), Gangeblova [Gangeblov's] (formerly the 13th), Knyazya Vyazemskago [Prince Vyazemskii's] (formerly the 14th), Shtedera [Steder's] (formerly the 15th), Shtempelya [Stempel's] (formerly the 16th), Likhacheva [Likhachev's] (formerly the 17th), Lazareva [Lazarev's] (formerly the 18th), Voeikova [Voeikov's] (formerly the 19th), and Kornitskago [Kornitskii] (formerly the 20th), each—of four battalions, and each battalion—of five companies.

VII.) Cuirassier Regiments [Kirasirskie polki]: Leib EGO VELICHESTVA [Life HIS MAJESTY'S], Leib EYA VELICHESTVA [Life HER MAJESTY'S], Knyazya Golitsyna 5-go [Prince Golitsyn 5th's] (formerly Voennago Ordena [of the Military Order]), Grafa Saltykova 2-go[Graf Saltykov 2nd's] (formerly theYekaterinoslavskii),Grafa Golovina [Graf Golovin's] (formerly theKazanskii), Brinkena [Brinken's](formerly the Glukhovskii),Zabolotskago [Zabolotskii's] (formerly the Kievskii),Voinova [Voinov's] (formerly the Starodubovskii),Musina-Pushkina [Musin-Pushkin's](formerly the Chernigovskii),Printsa Aleksandra Virtembergskago [Prince Alexander of Württemberg's] (formerly the Rizhskii [Riga]), Kozensa [Cozens's] (formerly the Kharkovskii), Knyazya Romadanovskago-Ladyzhenskago [Prince Romadanovskii-Ladyzhenskii's] (formerly the Malorossiiskii [Little Russia, or Ukraine]), and Tsorna[Zorn's] (formerly of the same name); each of five squadrons.

VIII.) Dragoon Regiments [Dragunskie polki]: Printsa Yevgeniya Virtembergskago [Prince Eugene of Württemberg's] (formerly the Pskovskii), Engelgardta[Engelhardt's] (formerly theS.-Peterburgskii), Michelsona 1-go [Mikhelson 1st's] (formerly the Smolenskii),Voevodskago [Voevodskii's](formerly the Orenburgskii), Khomyakova [Khomyakov's] (formerly the Ingermanlandskii [Ingermanland, or Ingria]),Bezobrazova Bezobrazov's] (formerly the Moskovskii [Moscow]),Grafa Palena 3-go [Graf Pahlen 3rd's](formerly the Kargopolskii),Miller 2-go [Müller 2nd's] (formerly Shreidersa [Schreider's]), Shepeleva [Shepelev's] (from the former Vladimirskii and Taganrogskii), Portnyagina [Portnyagin's] (from the former Narvskii and Nizhegorodskii [Narva and Nizhnii-Novgorod]), and Skalona[Skalon's] (from the former Irkutskii and Sibirskii [Siberia]); the last three—of ten squadrons, and the rest—of five.

IX.) Hussar Regiments [Gusarskie polki]: Boura [Bour's] (formerly the Pavlogradskii), Grafa Zubova[Graf Zubov's] (formerly the Sumskii [Sumy]), Melissino[Melissino's] (formerly the Mariupolskii), Kashinskago [Kashinskii's] (formerly the Aleksandrovskii), Grafa Palena 2-go [Graf Pahlen 2nd's] (formerly the Izyumskii), Borchugova [Borchugov's] (formerly the Akhtyrskii [Akhtyrka]), Sakena 3-go[Sacken 3rd's](formerly the Yelisavetgradskii), and Chaplygina [Chaplygin's] (formerly the Olviopolskii); each—of two five-squadron battalions.

XI.) Artillery Regiments [Artilleriiskie polki]: 1-i, 2-i, 3-i, 4-i, 5-i, 6-i, 7-i, and 8i; the last being horse [konnyi] and the rest foot [peshii]; each of five companies; Pionernyi polk [Pioneer Regiment]:—of two battalions, and a battalion—of one company of Miner-Sappers [Miner-Sapery] and five companies of Pioneers [Pionery]; and Pontonnyya Depo [Pontoon Depots]: the S.-Peterburgskoe, Rizhskoe [Riga], Smolenskoe, Kievskoe, Khersonskoe, Azovskoe, Kazanskoe, and Moskovskoe [Moscow].

XI.) Artillery Garrison Companies [Artilleriiskiya Garnizonnyya roty]: the Rochensalmskaya, Akhtiarskaya, Nikolaevskaya, and Kamenets-Podolskaya; and Garrison Artillery Commands [Garnizonnyya Artilleriiskiya komandy]: the Novodvinskaya, Neishlotskaya [Nyslott], Vilmanstrandskaya [Villmanstrand], Fridrikhsgamskaya [Fredrikshamn], Keksgolmskaya [Kexholm], Vyborgskaya [Viborg], S.-Peterburgskaya, Marientalskaya, Kronshtadtskaya [Kronstadt], Narvskaya [Narva], Pskovskaya, Velikolutskskaya [Velikie-Luki], Shlisselburgskaya [Schlüsselburg], Kazanskaya, Orenburgskaya, na Orenburgskoi linii [Orenburg, on the Orenburg Line], Gurevskaya, Tsaritsynskaya, Chernoyarskaya [Chernyi Yar], Astrakhanskaya, Yenotaevskaya, Krasnoyarskaya, Kizlyarskaya, Mozdokskaya, Kavkazskaya, na Kavkazskoi linii [Caucasus, on the Caucasian Line], Kievskaya, Ukrainskaya, Yelisavetgradskaya, Samarskaya [Samara], Dmitrievskaya, Ochakovskaya, Kinburnskaya, Tiraspolskaya, Khersonskaya, Taganrogskaya , Azovskaya, Yeiskaya, Petropavlovskaya, (u Azovskago morya) [Petropavlovsk, (on the Sea of Azov)], Aleksandrovskaya, Nikolaevskaya, Odesskaya [Odessa], v Korfu [in Corfu], Rizhskaya Tsitadelskaya [Riga Citadel], Rizhskaya Gorodovaya [Riga Town], Dinamindskaya [Dünamünde], Pernovskaya [Pernau], Arensburgskaya, Revelskaya, Baltiiskaya [Baltic (Port)], Smolenskaya, Tobolskaya, Selenginskaya, Nerchinskaya, Irkutskaya, Zhelezinskaya, Petropavlovskaya, (v kr. Sv. Petra) [Petropavlovsk, (in the St.-Peter Fortress)], Omskaya, Yamyshevskaya, Biiskaya, Semipalatnaya [Semipalatinsk], Ust-Kamenogorskaya, and Petropavlovskaya, (v Kamchatke) [Petropavlovsk, (in Kamchatka)].

XII.) Three Siege Depots of the Corps of Engineers [Tri Osadnyya Depo Inzhenernago Korpusa] and Fortress Engineer Commands [Krepostnyya Inzhenernyya komandy]: the Novodvinskaya, Neishlotskaya [Nyslott], Vilmandstrandskaya [Villmanstrand], Fridrikhsgamskaya [Fredrikshamn], Davydovskaya, Rochensalmskaya, Keksgolmskaya [Kexholm], Vyborgskaya [Viborg], S.-Petersburgskaya, Kronshtadtskaya [Kronstadt], Narvskaya [Narva], Shlisselburgskaya [Schlüsselburg], Orensburgkaya, Gurevskaya, Tsaritsynskaya, Chernoyarskaya [Chernyi Yar], Astrakhanskaya, Yenotaevskaya, Kizlyarskaya, Mozdokskaya, Ust-Labinskaya, Kavkazskaya, Georgievskaya, Kamenets-Podolskaya, Smolenskaya, Kievskaya, Azovskaya, Dmitrievskaya, Ochakovskaya, Kinburnskaya, Tiraspolskaya, Ovidiopolskaya, Perekopskaya, Akmechetskaya, Akhtiarskaya, Kerch-Yenikolskaya [Kerch-Yenikale], Fanagoriiskaya [Phanagoria], Khersonskaya, Odesskaya [Odessa], Moskovskaya [Moscow], Korfinskaya [Corfu], Rizhskaya [Riga], Dinamindskaya [Dünamünde], Pernovskaya [Pernau], Arensburgskaya, Revelskaya, Petropavlovskaya, (v, kr., Sv., Petra) [Petropavlovsk, (in the St.-Peter Fortress)], Omskaya, Irkutskaya, Selenginskaya, Yamyshevskaya [Yamyshevo], Zverinogolovskaya, Kefskaya [Kefe, or Kaffa], Biiskaya, Kuznetskaya, Semipalatnaya [Semipalatinsk], and Ust-Kamenogorskaya.

XIII.) Garrison Regiments [Garnizonnye polki]: Reikhenberga [Reichenberg's] (in Moscow) – of eight battalions; Bulgakova [Bulgakov's] (in Riga) – of four; Ukolova [Ukolov's] (in Kronstadt) – of four; Vyrubova 1-go [Vyrubov 1st's] (in Narva, Novgorod, Pskov, and Tver) – of four; Plutalova [Plutalov's] (in Schlüsselburg, Villmanstrand, Kexholm, and Nyslott) – of four; Essena 3-go [Essen 3rd's] (in Viborg and Fredrikshamn) – of four; Bolotnikova [Bolotnikov's] (in Rochensalm and Arensburg) – of four; Balasheva [Balashev's] (in Reval and Pernau) – of four; Knyzya Giki [Prince Gika's] (in Dünamünde, Smolensk, Vitebsk, and Mogilev) – of four; Masse [Masse's] (in Kiev and Kherson) – of four; Kosheleva [Koshelev's] (in Nikolaev, Perekop, and Sevastopol) – of four; Olvintseva [Olvintsev's] (in the St.-Dimitrii Fortress [kr. Sv. Dimitriya] and Azov) – of four; Leven 3-go [Leven 3rd's] (in Astrakhan, Tsaritsyn, and Simbirsk) – of four; Lebedeva [Lebedev's] (in Orenburg, Tambov, and Voronezh) – of four; Korfa 1-go [Korf 1st's] (in Saratov, the Orsk Fortress, Zverinogolovskoe, and Kizilsk Fortress) – of four; Tsyzyreva [Tsyzyrev's] (in Semipalatinsk, the St.-Peter Fortress, Verkhne-Uralsk, and the Troitsk Fortress) – of four; Retyunskago [Retyunskii's] (in Omsk, Biisk, Tomsk, and Zhelezinsk) – of four; Letstsano [Letstsano's] (in Irkutsk and Selenginsk) – of four; Pushchina 1-go [Pushchin 1st's] (in Kazan and Tobolsk) – of four; Livena 1-go [Liven 1st's] (in Archangel, Vladimir, and Nizhnii-Novgorod) – of four; Somova [Somov's] (in Nizhne-Kamchatsk) – of one, and Gogoleva [Gogolev's] (in the Corfu Fortress [krep. Korfu]) – of one; with the battalions—of five Musketeer companies, except the Archangel, Selenginsk, Nizhne-Kamchatsk, and Corfu garrisons, of which the first two consisted of two grenadier companies and the last two—of one; additionally, there were four such companies detached from the Omsk, Biisk Tomsk, and Zhelezinsk garrisons which made up a temporary combined battalion [vremennyi svodnyi batalion] in the town of Tara. The Astrakhan, Dimitrievsk, Narva, Novgorod, Pskov, Tver, Taganrog, Azov, Tsaritsyn, Simbirsk, Vladimir, and Nizhnii-Novgorod garrisons were maintained on an internal footing [vnutrennee polozhenie] while all the rest were on a field establishment [polevoe polozhenie].

XIV.) Invalid Companies [Invalidnyya roty], manned according to the personnel table [shtat] of 5 January, 1798, at garrisons on an internal establishment: Astrakhan, Dimitrievsk, Narva, Novgorod, Pskov, Tver, Taganrog, Azov, Tsaritsyn, Simbirsk, Vladimir, and Nizhnii-Novgorod: at Astrakhan – 3 companies, at Dimitrii – 2, and at the rest of the garrisons – 1 each.

XV.) Invalid Companies [Invalidnyya roty], remaining over and beyond the authorized strength [za shtatom], at garrisons which in 1798 and 1800 were transferred from an internal status to a field establishment: at Vitebsk, Mogilev, Tambov, and Voronezh – 1 company each, and at Tobolsk – 2 companies.

XVI.) Invalid Companies [Invalidnyya roty], remaining in towns and fortresses after the disbandment in 1800 of garrisons: at Kizlyar – 2 companies, and at Yelizavetgrad, Bakhmut, the Aleksandrovsk and Petrovsk fortresses, Sudak, Stavropol, Polotsk, Staryi-Bykhov, and Mozdok – 1 each.
XVII.) Invalid Company [Invalidnaya rota] in Bakhchisarai, moved there from Balaklava after the garrison battalion there was directed (3 September, 1799) to the Corfu Fortress.
XVIII.) Invalid Commands [Invalidnyya komandy], still left since 1796 and 1797 under the control of garrisons as over and beyond the authorized strength, one command each: at Moscow, Kronstadt, Villmanstrand, Kexholm, Fredrikshamn, Arensburg, Reval, Pernau, Dünamünde, Smolensk, Saratov, Orsk, Zverinogolovsk, Kizilsk, Semipalatinsk, Petrovsk, Verkhne-Uralsk, Troitsk, Omsk, Biisk, Tomsk, Zhelezinka, Irkutsk, and Selenginsk.

XIX.) Invalid Commands [Invalidnyya komandy], remaining, one each, after the disbandment in 1800 of garrisons at: the St.-Petersburg Fortress, Dünaburg [Dinaburg], and Baltic Port [Baltiiskii port].
XX.) Military-Educational Institutions [Voenno-Uchebnyya zavedeniya]: 1-i, 2-i, and Shklovskii Kadetskie korpusa [1st, 2nd, and Shklov Cadet Corps] and the Imperatorskii Voenno-Sirotskii dom [Imperial Military Orphans Home].

XXI.) Military Orphans Detachments [Voenno-Sirotskiya otdeleniya]: the S.-Peterburgskoe, Moskovskoe [Moscow], Narvskoe [Narva], Novgorodskoe, Arkhangelskoe, Nizhegorordskoe [Nizhnii-Novgorod], Tverskoe, Simbirskoe, Vladimirskoe, Tambovskoe, Smolenskoe, Pskovskoe, Kievskoe, Tsaritsynskoe, Kazanskoe, Verkhneuralskoe [Verkhne-Uralsk], Saratovskoe, Tobolskoe, Omskoe, Petropavlovskoe, Irkutskoe, Selenginskoe, Kronshtadtskoe

[Kronstadt], Shlisselburgskoe [Schlüsselburg], Rizhskoe [Riga], Revelskoe, Dinamindskoe [Dünamünde], Pernovskoe [Pernau], Arensburgskoe, Vitebskoe, Rogachevskoe, Vyborgskoe [Viborg], Fridrikhsgamskoe [Fredrikshamn], Vilmanstrandskoe [Villmanstrand], Keksgolmskoe [Kexholm], Neishlotskoe [Nyslott], Khersonskoe, Taganrogskoe, Balaklavskoe [Balaklava], Nikitinskoe, Kirilovskoe [Kirillov], Perekopskoe, Astrakhanskoe, Dimitrievskoe, Azovskoe, Orenburgskoe, Orskoe, Kizilskoe, Troitskoe, Zverinogolovskoe, Biiskoe, Tomskoe, Semipalatinskoe, and Nizhne-Kamchatskoe.

XXII.) Regular Cossack Troops [Regulyarnyya Kazachi voiska]: the Chuguevskii polk [Chuguev Regiment], 1-i and 2-i Teptyarskie polki [1st and 2nd Teptyar Regiments], and Leib-Uralskaya sotnya [Life-Ural Sotnia].

XXIII.) Irregular Cossack Hosts [Irregulyarnyya Kazachi voiska]: the Donskoe, Chernomorskoe [Black Sea], Sibirskoe [Siberian], Orenburgskoe, Uralskoe, and Astrakhanskoe.

XXIV.) Settled Caucasian Cossacks [Poselennye Kavkazskie kazaki]: the Grebenskie, Terskie [Terek], Semeinye [Family], Khoperskie, Volzhskie [Volga], Kizlyarskie, and Mozdokskie, and the Stavropolskie kreshchenye Kalmyki [Stavropol baptized Kalmucks].

XXV.) National Troops [Natsionalnyya voiska]: the Gorskaya Mozdokskaya komanda [Mozdok Mountaineer Command], Balaklavskii Grecheskii pekhotnyi batalion [Balaklava Greek Infantry Battalion], Litovskii-Tatarskii Glovenskago polk [Glovenskii's Lithuanian-Tatar Regiment], and Polskii konnyi Knyazya Ratieva polk [Prince Ratiev's Polish Horse Regiment]; the second—of four companies, and the rest—of ten squadrons.

XXVI.) Mines [Gornozavodskie]: the Kolyvano-Voskresenskii and Nerchinskii bataliony; two companies at the Yekaterinburg gold works; two companies at the Goroblagodatsk and Kamsk mines and one at the Olonetsk-Petrovsk works.

XXVII.) Commands of Non-Serving Invalids [Komandy nesluzhashchikh invalidov]: the L.-Gv. [Life-Guards], Muromskaya, Kasimovskaya, Arzamasskaya, Shatskaya, Tambovskaya, Penzinskaya [Penza], Lebedyanskaya, Kozmodemyanskaya, Kadomskaya, Alatyrskaya, Temnikovskaya, Kerenskaya, Saranskaya, Nizhnelomovskaya [Nizhnii-Lomov], Insarskaya, Putivlskaya, Pronskaya, Kozelskaya, Ryazhskaya, Bezhetskaya, Zaraiskaya, Syzranskaya, Urzhumskaya, Yadrinskaya, Kurmyshskaya, Slobodskaya, Kozlovskaya, Sviyazhskaya, Verkhnelomovskaya [Verkhnyi-Lomov], and Vyatskaya [Vyatka].

XXVIII.) State Companies [Shtatnyya roty] in provincial [gubernskii] towns and State Commands [Shtatnyya komandy] in district [uezdnyi] towns: in St.-Petersburg Province [guberniya] – 7, in Moscow – 11, in Novgorod – 12, in Tver – 9, in Pskov – 6, in Smolensk – 9, in Tula – 9, in Kaluga – 9, in Yaroslavl – 9, in Kostroma – 9, in Vladimir – 10, in Nizhnii-Novgorod – 10, in Vologda – 10, in Archangel – 8, in Vyatka – 10, in Kazan – 10, in Perm – 12, in Orenburg – 10, in Simbirsk – 10, in Penza – 10, in Astrakhan – 10, in Voronezh – 10, in Saratov – 10, in Tambov – 10, in Ryazan – 9, in Kursk – 10, in Orel – 10, in Slobodsko-Urkraina – 10, in New Russia [Novorossiiskaya guberniya] – 12, in Little Russia [Malorossiiskaya guberniya] – 12, in Minsk – 10, in Belorussia [Belorusskaya guberniya] – 16, in Volhynia – 12, in Podolia – 12, in Kiev – 12, in Lithuania [Litovskaya guberniya]– 19, in Courland [Kurlyandskaya guberniya] – 8, in Viborg – 6, in Estonia [Estlyandskaya guberniya] – 4, in Livonia [Liflyandskaya guberniya]– 5, in Tobolsk – 16, and in Irkutsk – 17.

Such were the military land forces of Russia upon the death of Emperor Paul I. During the twenty-five year reign of Emperor Alexander I, noteworthy both for its great military events and the important improvements in the internal and external composition of the military structure, the numerous and varied forces of the Russian Empire underwent the following changes in their composition and nomenclature:

I. ARMY INFANTRY (SECOND PART ON VOLUME 9)

16 March 1801–The Mushketerskii General-Maiora Knyzya Vyazemskago polk (formerly the Tomskii) is named the Mushketerskii General-Maiora Stellikha polk [Major General Stellikh's Musketeer Regiment] (1) .

29 March 1801– All Grenadier, Musketeer, and Jäger regiments, named after their chefs, are renamed:

a) Grenadier Regiments:

Kerbitsa (formerly the Pavlovskii) — as the Pavlovskii Grenaderskii polk.   Palitsyna (formerly the Yekaternoslavskii, then the Pskovskii) — as the Yekaterinoslavskii.   Sakena 1-go (formerly the S.-Peterburgskii) — as the S.-Peterburgskii.

Naslednago Printsa Meklenburgskago (formerly the Astrakhanskii) — as the Astrakhanskii.

Passeka (formerly the Kievskii) — as the Kievskii.   Printsa Meklenburgskago Karla (formerly the Moskovskii) — as the Moskovskii.   Berkha (formerly the Malorossiiskii) — as the Malorossiiskii.

Bakhmeteva 3-go (formerly the Sibirskii) — as the Sibirskii.   Mamaeva(formerly the Fanagoriiskii) — as the Fanagoriiskii.   Titova 1-go (formerly the Khersonskii) — as the Khersonskii.   Danzasa (formerly the Tavricheskii) — as the Tavricheskii.   Tuchkova 2-go (formerly the Kavkazskii) — as the Kavkazskii.

b) Musketeer Regiments:

Sedmoratskago (formerly the Belozerskii) — as the Belozerskii Mushketerskii polk   Yermolova (formerly the Nasheburgskii) — as the Nasheburgskii.

Essena 1-go (formerly the Chernigovskii) — as the Chernigovskii.

Barona Rozena (formerly the Novoingermanlandskii) — as the Novoingermanlandskii.

Lasunskago 1-go (formerly the Yaroslavskii) — as the Yaroslavskii.

Miloradovicha 1-go (formerly the Apsheronskii) — as the Apsheronskii.

Repninskago (formerly the Smolenskii) — as the Smolenskii.

Grafa Lanzherona (formerly the Ryazhskii) — as the Ryazhskii.

Prshibyshevskago (formerly the Kurskii) — as the Kurskii.

Maksheeva (formerly the Kozlovskii) — as the Kozlovskii.

Serbina (formerly the Sevastopolskii) — as the Sevastopolskii.

Mansurova (formerly the Belevskii) — as the Belevskii.

Lidersa (formerly the Bryanskii) — as the Bryanskii.

Izmailova (formerly the Shlisselburgskii) — as the Shlisselburgskii.

Loveiki (formerly the Aleksopolskii) — as the Aleksopolskii.

Borozdina 2-go (formerly the Troitskii) — as the Troitskii.

Sukina 2-go (formerly the Ladozhskii) — as the Ladozhskii.

Tinkova (formerly the Polotskii) — as the Polotskii.

Grafa Kamenskago (formerly the Arkhangelogorodskii) — as the Arkhangelogorodskii.

Engelgardta (formerly the Staroingermanlandskii) — as the Staroingermanlandskii.

Fertcha (formerly the Novgorodskii) — as the Novgorodskii.

Khitrovo (formerly the Nizhegorodskii) — as the Nizhegorodskii.

Musina-Pushkina (formerly the Vitebskii) — as the Vitebskii.

Selekhova (formerly the Azovskii) — as the Azovskii.

Brunova (formerly the Orlovskii) — as the Orlovskii.

Khotuntseva (formerly the Revelskii) — as the Revelskii.

Drekselya (formerly the Tulskii) — as the Tulskii.

Yefimovicha (formerly the Yeletskii) — as the Yeletskii.

Golenishcheva-Kutuzova (formerly the Pskovskii) — as the Pskovskii.

Fershtera (formerly the Tambovskii) — as the Tambovskii.

Mitskago (formerly the Rostovskii) — as the Rostovskii.

Petrovskago (formerly the Muromskii) — as the Muromskii.

Bykova (formerly the Staroskolskii) — as the Staroskolskii.

Garina (formerly the Tobolskii) — as the Tobolskii.

Leonteva (formerly the Tiflisskii) — as the Tiflisskii.

Arseneva (formerly the Voronezhskii) — as the Voronezhskii.

Knorringa 2-go (formerly the Kazanskii) — as the Kazanskii.

Fensha (formerly the Moskovskii) — as the Moskovskii.

Gulyakova (formerly the Kabardinskii) — as the Kabardinskii.

Rozenberga (formerly the Vladimirskii) — as the Vladimirskii.

Gersdorfa (formerly the Uglitskii) — as the Uglitskii.

Tuchkova 1-go (formerly the Sevskii) — as the Sevskii.
Rodgofa (formerly the Narvskii) — as the Narvskii.
Konovicha (formerly the Dneprovskii) — as the Dneprovskii.
Manteifelya (formerly the Vyatskii) — as the Vyatskii.
Shenshina (formerly the Suzdalskii) — as the Suzdalskii.
Verderevskago (formerly the Keksgolmskii) — as the Keksgolmskii.
Ganzhi (formerly the Vyborgskii) — as the Vyborgskii.
Alekseeva (formerly the Ryazanskii) — as the Ryazanskii.
Knyazya Gorchakova 2-go (formerly the Nevskii) — as the Nevskii.
Kastelliya (formerly the Velikolutskii) — as the Velikolutskii.
Nechaeva (formerly the Sofiiskii) — as the Sofiiskii.
Lavrova (formerly the Shirvanskii) — as the Shirvanskii.
Barona Vimpfena (formerly the Permskii) — as the Permskii.
Shembeka (formerly the Nizovskii) — as the Nizovskii.
Malyshkina (formerly the Butyrskii) — as the Butyrskii.
Bakhmeteva 1-go (formerly the Rylskii) — as the Rylskii.
Tsybulskago (formerly the Ufimskii) — as the Ufimskii.
Pevtsova (formerly the Yekaterinburgskii) — as the Yekaterinburgskii.
Stellikha (formerly the Tomskii) — as the Tomskii.
Kupfershmita (formerly the Selenginskii) — as the Selenginskii.
Knyazya Shcherbatova (formerly Arkharova 1-go) — as the Tenginskii.
Runicha (formerly Pavlutskago) — as the Navaginskii.
Nesvetaeva (formerly Leitnera) — as the Saratovskii.
Kashkina (formerly Branta) — as the Olonetskii.
Millera 1-go(formerly of the same name) — as the Kolyvanskii.
Anikeeva (formerly Marklovicha 1-go) — as the Poltavskii.
Baklanovskago (formerly Berkha) — as the Ukrainskii.
Ushakova (formerly the Senatskii) — as the Litovskii.

c) Jäger Regiments:

Mikhelsona (formerly the 2-i) — as the Pervyi Yegerskii polk [First Jäger Regiment].
Gvozdeva (formerly the 3-i) — as the Vtoroi [Second].
Barklaya-de-Tolli (formerly the 4-i) — as the Tretii [Third].
Bradke (formerly the 5-i) — as the Chetvertyi [Fourth].
Alfimova (formerly the 6-i) — as the Pyatyi [Fifth].
Grafa Ivelicha 3-go (formerly the 7-i) — as the Shestoi [Sixth].
Millera 3-go (formerly the 8-i) — as the Sedmoi [Seventh].
Priudy (formerly the 9-i) — as the Vosmoi [Eighth].
Veidemeiera (formerly the 10-i) — as the Devyatyi [Ninth].
Markova 2-go (formerly the 11-i) — as the Desyatyi [Tenth].
Bally (formerly the 12-i) — as theOdinnadtsatyi [Eleventh].
Gangeblova (formerly the 13-i) — as theDvenadtsatyi [Twelfth].
Knyazya Vyazemskago (formerly the 14-i) — as theTrinadtsatyi [Thirteenth].
Shtedera (formerly the 15-i) — as theChetyrnadtsatyi [Fourteenth].
Shtempelya (formerly the 16-i) — as thePyatnadtsatyi [Fifteenth].
Likhacheva 1-go (formerly the 17-i) — as theShestnadtsatyi [Sixteenth].
Lazareva (formerly the 18-i) — as the Semnadtsatyi [Seventeenth].
Voeikova (formerly the 19-i) — as theVosemnadtsatyi [Eighteenth].
Kornitskago (formerly the 20-i) — as theDevyatnadtsatyi [Nineteenth] (2).
All these regiments were assigned to the following fourteen Inspectorates [Inspektsii]:

IN THE FINLYANDSKAYA [FINLAND]INSPEKTSIYA — Velikie-Luki, Neva, and Ryazan Musketeers, and 1st and 2nd Jägers.
—S.-PETERBURGSKAYA — Life and Pavlovsk Grenadiers; Yelets, Kexholm, Belozersk, Tenginsk, and Lithuania [Litovskii] Musketeers.
—LIFLYANDSKAYA [LIVONIA]— St.-Petersburg and Taurica Grenadiers; Sevsk, Sofiya, Reval, Tobolsk, Dnieper, and Chernigov Musketeers, and 3rd Jägers.

—LITOVSKAYA [LITHUANIA]— Yekaterinoslavl Grenadiers; Tula, Pskov, Murom, Rostov, Nizovsk, and Archangel Musketeers, and 4th, 5th, 6th, and 7th Jägers.

—BRESTSKAYA — Old Ingermanland, Ryazhsk, Viborg, Apsheron, and Azov Musketeers, and 8th Jägers.—UKRAINSKAYA — Little Russia and Kiev Grenadiers, and Smolensk and Bryansk Musketeers.

—DNESTROVSKAYA [DNIESTER]— Kherson and Siberia Grenadiers; Ladoga, Vladimir, New Ingermanland, Aleksopol, Kozlov, Yaroslavl, and Nizhnii-Novgorod   Musketeers, and 9th, 10th, 11th, 12th and 13th Jägers.

—KRYMSKAYA [CRIMEA] INSPEKTSIYA — Belev, Sevastopol, Troitsk, and Vitebsk Musketeers, and 14th and 15th Jägers.

—KAVKAZSKAYA [CAUCASUS]— Caucasus Grenadiers; Suzdal, Tiflis, Karbarda, and Caucasus Musketeers, and 16th and 17th Jägers.

—SMOLENSKAYA — Moscow and Phanagoria Grenadiers, and Polotsk, Perm, Uglich, Kursk, and Voronezh Musketeers.

—KIEVSKAYA — Moscow, Butyrskii, Kolyvan, Novgorod, Vyatka, Narva, and Poltava Musketeers.

—MOSKOVSKAYA [MOSCOW]— Astrakhan Grenadiers and Navaginsk, Tambov, Ukraine, Schlüsselburg, Nasheburg, Orel, Saratov, Staryi-Oskol, and Olonets Musketeers.

—ORENBURGSKAYA — Rylsk, Ufa, and Yekaterinburg Musketeers.

—SIBIRSKAYA [SIBERIA]— Shirvan, Tomsk, and Selenginsk Musketeers, and 18th and 19th Jägers (3).

30 April 1802– All Army infantry regiments are ordered to consist of three four-company battalions: the Life Grenadiers – of three Grenadier battalions; other Grenadiers – of one Grenadier and two Fusilier [Fuzelernyi] battalions; Musketeers – of one Grenadier and two Musketeer battalions; Jägers – of three Jäger battalions (4).

29 December 1802– a new Musketeer regiment is established, called the Kurinskii [Kura]Mushketerskii polk and coming under the Moscow Inspectorate, while from this last the Saratov Musketeers are transferred to the Caucasus Inspectorate (5).

16 May 1803– New regiments are established: the Petrovskii, Koporskii [Kopore], Volynskii [Volhynia], Podolskii [Podolia], Galitskii [Galich], Krymskii [Crimea], and Vologodskii [Vologda]Mushketerskie polki, and the 20-i Yegerskii polk, assigned to Inspectorates:

Petrovsk to the St.-Petersburg Inspectorate.
Kopore— Livonia.
Volhynia— Lithuania.
Podolia— Brest.
Galich— Ufa [sic, should be Ukraine – M.C.].
Crimea— Dniester.
Vologda — Caucasus.
20th Jägers— St.-Petersburg (6).

29 August 1805– Still more new regiments are established: the Mogilevskii, Kaluzhskii [Kaluga], Kostromskii [Kostroma], Vilenskii [Vilna], Penzinskii [Penza], Estlyandskii [Estonia], and Odesskii [Odessa]Mushketerskie polki, and the 21-i and 22-i Yegerskie polki, assigned to Inspectorates:

Kaluga to the Livonia Inspectorate.
Mogilev— Lithuania.
Kostroma— Lithuania.
Vilna— Brest.
Penza — Brest.
Estonia — Ukraine.
Odessa— Livonia.
21st Jägers— Caucasus.
22nd Jägers — Dniester (7).

1 March 1806– The 23-i Yegerskii polk is established (8).

4 May 1806– From the forces of the Finland, St.-Petersburg, Livonia, Lithuania, Brest, Ukraine, Dniester, Crimea, Smolensk, Kiev, and Moscow inspectorates are formed 13 divisions [divizii], to which went, from the regiments of army infantry:

In the 1st Division—Life-Grenadiers; Kexholm, Velikie-Luki, Neva, and Petrovsk Musketeers; 2nd Jägers.
    —2nd -St.-Petersburg and Pavlovsk Grenadiers; Belozersk, Ryazan, Rostov, Yelets, and Lithuania Musketeers; 1st Jägers.
    —3rd -Taurica Grenadiers; Chernigov, Murom, and Kopore Musketeers; 21st Jägers.
    —4th - Dniester, Tula, Tenginsk, Navaginsk, Tobolsk, and Polotsk Musketeers; 4th Jägers.
    —5th - Uglich, Sofiya, Perm, Mogilev, Kaluga, and Sevsk Musketeers; 20th Jägers.

—6th -Kostroma, Nizovsk, Reval, Vilna, Volhynia, and Staryi-Oskol Musketeers; 3rd Jägers.

—7th - Yekaterinoslavl Grenadiers; Vladimir, Pskov, Azov, Voronezh, and Moscow Musketeers; 5th Jägers.

— 8th - Moscow Grenadiers; Viborg, Schlüsselburg, Old Ingermanland, Archangel, and Podolia Musketeers; 7th Jägers.

—9th - Astrakhan Grenadiers; Tambov, Orel, Ukraine, Crimea, Penza, and Galich Musketeers; 10th Jägers.

—10th - Kiev Grenadiers; Ryazhsk, Yaroslavl, Bryansk, Kursk, and Vyatka Musketeers; 6th Jägers.

—11th -Little Russia and Siberia Grenadiers; Odessa, Olonets, Apsheron, and Nasheburg Musketeers;11th Jägers.

—12th - Phanagoria Grenadiers; New Ingermanland, Narva, Novgorod, Smolensk, and Butyrskii Musketeers; 8th Jägers.

—13th - Estonia, Ladoga, Poltava, Nizhnii-Novgorod, and Aleksopol Musketeers; 12th and 22nd Jägers.

The rest of the regiments were included in these Inspectorates:

—In the KAVKAZSKAYA [CAUCASUS]— Caucasus and Kherson Grenadiers; Kazan, Suzdal, Tiflis, Karbarda, Sevastopol, Saratov, Vologda, Troitsk, and Belev Musketeers, and 9th, 15th, 16th and 17th Jägers.

—ORENBURGSKAYA — Rylsk, Ufa, and Yekaterinburg Musketeers.

—SIBIRSKAYA [SIBERIA]— Shirvan, Tomsk, and Selenginsk Musketeers, and 18th and 19th Jägers.

The 23rd Jäger Regiment, because of its still incomplete formation, and the Kozlov, Vitebsk, Kolyvan, and Kura Musketeers and the 13th and 14th Jägers, since they were outside the country in the Mediterranean Sea, were left not included in any of the divisions, pending further directions (9).

13 June 1806 – Additional Yegerskie polki are established: the 24-i,25-i,and 26-i (10).

14 June 1806 – One more division, the 14-ya, was added to the 13 already formed, and to which were assigned from the regiments of Army infantry: from the 2nd Division– the Belozersk and Ryazan Musketeers; from the 5th Division – the Uglich and Sofiya Musketeers; and from the newly formed Jäger regiments – the 23rd and 26th. The 24th Jägers were assigned to the 2nd Division, and the 25th—to the 5th Division, and consequently the following Grenadier, Musketeer, and Jäger regiments were in the 2nd, 5th, and 14th divisions (11):

In the 2nd Division: Pavlovsk Grenadiers.
      Rostov Musketeers.
      St.-Petersburg Grenadiers.
      Yelets Musketeers.
      1st Jägers.
      24th

— 5th ———: Perm Musketeers.
      Mogilev
      Kaluga
      Sevsk
      20th Jägers.
      25th

— 14th ——: Belozersk Musketeers.
      Ryazan
      Uglich
      Sofiya
      23rd Jägers.
      26th

24 June 1806 – Seventeen more regiments were established: the Brestkii,Kremenchugskii,Minskii,Neishlotskii [Nyslott],Yakutskii,Okhotskii,Kamchatskii [Kamchatka],Mingrelskii [Mingrelia],Vilmanstrandskii [Villmanstrand],Libavskii [Libau], and Pernovskii [Pernau]Mushketerskii polki, and the27-i,28-i,29-i,30-i,31-i,and32-i Yegerskie polki. With the expansion of the Army by these regiments, four new divisions were formed: the 15-ya, 16-ya, 17-ya, and 18-ya, in which were included the following regiments:

In the 15th Division: Kozlov, Vitebsk, Kura, and Kolyvan Musketeers, and 13th and 14th Jägers.

— 16th ———: Petrovsk, Libau, Kamchatka, and Mingrelia Musketeers, and 27th and 28th Jägers.

— 17th ———: Villmanstrand, Brest, Kremenchug, and Minsk Musketeers, and 30th and 31st Jägers.

— 18th ———: Tambov, Yakutsk, Nyslott, and Okhotsk Musketeers, and 29th and 32nd Jägers.

The Pernau Musketeer Regiment went to the 1st Division (12).

In February 1807– The name "Caucasus Inspectorate" was abolished, and in its place were established the 19-ya and 20-ya divizii, which included the following regiments:

In the 19th Division: Kazan, Suzdal, Vologda, Belev, and Sevastopol Musketeers, and 16th and 17th Jägers.

— 20th : Kherson and Caucasus Grenadiers; Kabarda, Troitsk, Tiflis, and Saratov Musketeers; and 9th and 15th Jägers (13).

In June 1807– With the inclusion of the Guards infantry regiments in the 1st Division, the Velikie-Luki, Neva, and Petrovsk Musketeers and the 2nd Jägers, which had been in that division, formed, along with Libau Musketeers from the 16th Division, the 21-ya diviziya. To replace of the Libau Regiment came the Novgorod, transferred from the 12th Division (14). Along with this, the Vyatka Regiment from the 10th Division, the Staryi-Oskol from the 11th, the Olonets from the 11th, the Viborg from the 8th, the Penza from the 9th, and the 29th Jägers, were all reassigned to the 22-ya diviziya (15).

5 February 1808– The Orenburg Inspectorate was renamed the 23-ya diviziya, and the Siberia Inspectorate—24-ya. The first consisted of the Rylsk, Ufa, and Yekaterinburg Regiments; the second—of the Shirvan, Tomsk, and Selenginsk, and the 18th and 19th Jägers (16).

12 August 1808– In honor of the courageous defense of the Danzig fortress, from the three combined Garrison battalions which were there it was ordered to form an Army regiment titled the Belostokskii Mushketerskii polk [Bialystok Musketeer Regiment], to be part of the 9th Division (17).

30 October 1808– In order to avoid the deficiencies connected with the hasty distribution of recruits to regiments after their enlistment, for their call-up there were established, in various places corresponding to the permanent deployment of troops in their quarters, Replacement Recruit Depots [Zapasnyya Rekrutskiya Depo], each consisting of six infantry companies (18). It was proposed to establish these depots in: Tikhvin, Kholm, Toropets, Zaslavl, Roslavl, Ivenets, Rovno, Chudnov, Novomirgorod, Novgorod-Severskii, Olviopol, Kharkov, Yekaterinoslavl, Staraya-Russa, Glukhov, Bryansk, Yaroslavl, Vladimir, Ivanovo, Dmitrievsk, Olonets, Akhtyrka, Ufa, Tara, Kargopol, Nizhnii-Novogorod, Dmitrovsk, Tetyushi, and Belogorodka (the small town in Kiev Province) (19); but due to difficulties encountered, the mustering of recruits in Tikhvin, Dmitrievsk, Ufa, and Tara was canceled and in their place it was directed to have two depots: in Azov and Korostyn [Korosten] (20).

5 April 1809– Regiments were reassigned from one division to another:
From the 4th Division to the 6th:Tenginsk and Tula Musketeers.
— 4th — — — 17th: Polotsk and Navaginsk Musketeers.
— 6th — — — 4th: Vilna and Volhynia Musketeers.
— 17th — — — 4th: Kremenchug and Minsk Musketeers.

After these transfers, the following regiments of Army infantry were part of the 4th Division: the Kremenchug, Minsk, Tobolsk, Volhynia, and Vilna Musketeers, and the 4th Jägers (21).

12 August 1809– It was directed that a part of the recruits in each Recruit Depot be held for the cavalry (22).

29 September 1809– The Life-Grenadier and the Kexholm Musketeer regiments were assigned to the 1st or Guards Division [1-ya ili Gvardeiskaya diviziya], and twenty-four divisions, divided into brigades [brigady], were formed from the rest of the regiments:

2nd Division   1st Brigade: St.-Petersburg Grenadiers and Yelets Musketeers.
     2nd — — Pavlovsk Grenadiers and Polotsk Musketeers.
     3rd — — Lithuania Musketeers and 1st Jägers.
3rd — — 1st — — Taurica Grenadiers and Chernigov Musketeers.
     2nd — — Murom and Kopore Musketeers.
     3rd — — 20th and 21st Jägers.
4th — — 1st — — Kremenchug and Minsk Musketeers.
     2nd — — Tobolsk and Volhynia Musketeers.
     3rd — — Vilna Musketeers and 4th Jägers.
5th — — 1st — — Sevsk and Kaluga Musketeers.
     2nd — — Perm and Mogilev Musketeers.
     3rd — — 23rd and 24th Jägers.
6th — — 1st — — Nizovsk and Azov Musketeers.
     2nd — — Uglich and Reval Musketeers.
     3rd — — Sofia Musketeers and 3rd Jägers.
7th — — 1st — — Yekaterinoslavl Grenadiers and Moscow Musketeers.
     2nd — — Pskov and Vladimir Musketeers.
     3rd — — Podolia Musketeers and 5th Jägers.
8th — — 1st — — Moscow Grenadiers and Archangel Musketeers.
     2nd — — Schlüsselburg and Old Ingermanland Musketeers.
     3rd — — Voronezh Musketeers and 7th Jägers.
9th — — 1st — — Astrakhan Grenadiers and Bialystok Musketeers.
     2nd — — Ryazhsk and Ukraine Musketeers.
     3rd — — Galich Musketeers and 10th Jägers.

10th ——	1st ——	Kiev Grenadiers and Crimea Musketeers.
	2nd ——	Kursk and Yaroslavl Musketeers.
	3rd ——	Bryansk Musketeers and 8th Jägers.
11th ——	1st ——	Little Russia Grenadiers and Apsheron Musketeers.
	2nd ——	Siberia Grenadiers and Nasheburg Musketeers.
	3rd ——	Odessa Musketeers and 11th Jägers.
12th ——	1st ——	Phanagoria Grenadiers and New Ingermanland Musketeers.
	2nd ——	Smolensk and Narva Musketeers.
	3rd ——	Orel Musketeers and 6th Jägers.
13th ——	1st ——	Nizhnii-Novgorod and Ladoga Musketeers.
	2nd ——	Aleksopol and Butyrskii Musketeers.
	3rd ——	Poltava and Estonia Musketeers.
	4th ——	12th and 22nd Jägers.
14th ——	1st ——	Graf Arakcheev's and Tenginsk Musketeers.
	2nd ——	Tula and Navaginsk Musketeers.
	3rd ——	25th and 26th Jägers.
15th ——	1st ——	Kozlov and Vitebsk Musketeers.
	2nd ——	Kura and Kolyvan Musketeers.
	3rd ——	13th and 14th Jägers.
16th ——	1st ——	Okhotsk and Nyslott Musketeers.
	2nd ——	Kamchatka and Mingrelia Musketeers.
	3rd ——	Novgorod Musketeers and 27th Jägers.
17th ——	1st ——	Ryazan and Bialystok [sic, should be Belozersk] Musketeers.
	2nd ——	Villmanstrand and Brest Musketeers.
	3rd ——	30th and 31st Jägers.
18th ——	1st ——	Tambov and Yakutsk Musketeers.
	2nd ——	Kostroma and Dnieper Musketeers.
	3rd ——	28th and 32nd Jägers.
19th ——	1st ——	Kazan and Suzdal Musketeers.
	2nd ——	Belev and Sevastopol Musketeers.
	3rd ——	Vologda Musketeers and 16th and 17th Jägers.
20th ——	1st ——	Caucasus and Kherson Grenadiers.
	2nd——	Troitsk and Tiflis Musketeers.
	3rd ——	Kabarda and Saratov Musketeers.
	4th ——	9th and 15th Jägers.
21st ——	1st ——	Neva and Petrovsk Musketeers.
	2nd ——	Libau and Pernau Musketeers.
	3rd ——	Velikie-Luki Musketeers and 2nd Jägers.
22nd ——	1st ——	Vyatka and Staryi-Oskol Musketeers.
	2nd ——	Olonets and Viborg Musketeers.
	3rd ——	Penza Musketeers and 29th Jägers.
23rd ——	(of one brig.)	Rylsk and Yekaterinburg Musketeers.
24th ——	(of one brig.)	Selenginsk Musketeers and 18th Jägers.
25th ——	1st Brigade:	Ufa and Shirvan Musketeers.
	2nd ——	Tomsk Musketeers and 19th Jagers (23).

12 October 1810– Regiments of Army infantry were ordered to make the following changes in their organization:

1.) In each Grenadier regiment (except the Life-Grenadiers), instead of one Grenadier and two Fusilier battalions, there were to be three Fusilier battalions, of one Grenadier and three Fusilier companies.

2.) In each Musketeer regiment, instead of one Grenadier and two Musketeer battalions, there were to be three Musketeer battalions, of one Grenadier and three Musketeer companies.

3.) In each Jäger regiment the battalions were to consist of one Grenadier and three Musketeer companies.

4.) In each Fusilier, Musketeer, and Jäger battalion, the senior, or Grenadier, company was to be made up of grenadiers and marksmen [strelki], so that the grenadiers are in the first platoon [vzvod] and marksmen in the second.

5.) When regiments are in battle formation, the 1st, or Grenadier, platoon of the Grenadier company was to deploy on the right flank of its battalion, while the 2nd, or Marksmen [Strelkovyi] platoon, was to be on the left.

6.) During wartime, when regiments move out on campaign, the Fusilier, Musketeer, and Jäger companies of the second battalions, having been used to fill up the other two battalions, were to remain in their quarters and were to be termed Replacement [Zapasnyi] battalions.

7.) The Grenadier companies of second battalions were to set out on campaign with the first and third battalions.

8.) When all six regiments of a division were united together, the Grenadier companies of their second battalions were to form for it two Combined Grenadier Battalions [Svodnye Grenaderskie bataliony], each of three companies.

9.) In each Corps [Korpus], the Combined Grenadier Battalions were to form a Combined Grenadier Brigade [Svodnaya Grenaderskaya brigada] and be the Reserve [Rezerv] of this Corps.

10.) In an Army [Armiya], the Combined Grenadier Brigades of its Corps were to form a Combined Grenadier Division [Svodnaya Grenaderskaya diviziya] and be its Reserve(24).

19 October 1810 – Certain Musketeer regiments were titled Jägers: the Lithuania– as the 33rd, Vilna– as the 34th, Sofiya– as the 35th, Podolia– as the 36th, Voronezh– as the 37th, Galich– as the 38th, Bryansk– as the 39th, Odessa– as the 40th, Orel– as the 41st, Estonia– as the 42nd, Novgorod– as the 43rd, Velikie-Luki– as the 44th, Penza– as the 45th, and Saratov– as the 46th. This change in titles was done so that in all divisions there would be two Jäger regiments, and with this the following brigades were ordered to be made up of the indicated regiments:

        4th Div. 2nd Brigade — of the Tobolsk and Volhynia Musketeers.
              3rd ——— — 4th and 34th Jägers.
        7th —— 2nd ——— — Pskov and Vladimir Musketeers.
              3rd ——— — 5th and 36th Jägers.
        8th —— 1st ——— — Moscow Grenadiers and Archangel Musketeers.
              3rd ——— — 7th and 37th Jägers.
        9th —— 1st ——— — Astrakhan Grenadiers and Bialystok Musketeers.
              3rd ——— — 10th and 38th Jägers.
        11th —— 1st——— — Little Russia Grenadiers and Apsheron Musketeers.
              3rd ——— — 11th and 40th Jägers.
        13th —— 3rd ——— — 12th and 22nd Jägers (25).

26 October 1810 – With the establishment of Corps [Korpusa], they were composed of the Army Infantry regiments of the following divisions:

        In the 1st Corps, regiments of the 5th and 14th Divisions.
              2nd ————— 16th, 17th, and 21st Divisions.
              3rd ————— 2nd, 3rd, and 4th Divisions.
              4th ————— 7th and 25th Divisions, and replacement or second battalions of regiments of the 9th, 10th and 18th Divisions.
              6th ————— 19th and 20th Divisions.

The composition of the 5th Corps was not laid down (26).

31 October 1810 – The changes effected on 12 October for the organization of Grenadier regiments were extended to the Life-Grenadiers, with the distinction that for that regiment all companies were titled Grenadiers (27).

3 November 1810 – The 25th Division was renamed the 24th, and the regiments which made up the latter (Rylsk, Yekaterinburg, and Selenginsk Musketeers and 18th Jägers) were left, until specially directed, under the authority of their Brigade Commanders (28).

10 November 1810 – The 2nd Battalion of the Yelets Musketeer Regiment was designated for Military Settlement [Voennoe Poselenie] in Mogilev Province, Klimovetsk District [povet], in the Bobylets tract [starostvo], and consequently took the title of Settled [Poselenyi] Battalion of the Yelets Musketeer Regiment (29).

17 January 1811 – From various Garrison regiments and battalions designated for disbandment, Army regiments were established: the Voronezhskii, Bryanskii, Litovskii [Lithuania], Podolskii [Podolia], Estlyandskii [Estonia], Orlovskii [Orel], Galitskii [Galich], Velikolutskii [Velikie-Luki], Penzinskii [Penza], and Saratovskii Pekhotnye [Infantry], and the 47-i, 48-i, and 49-i Yegerskie [Jägers], and consequently various of the divisions were ordered to reorganize:

        1st Division   — of the Life, Pavlovsk, St.-Petersburg, Yekaterinoslavl, and Taurica Grenadiers, and Graf Arakcheev's Musketeers.
              13th ——— — Galich, Velikie-Luki, Penza, and Saratov Infantry, and the 12th and 22nd Jägers.
              25th ——— — 1st, 2nd, and 3rd Marines [Morskie]*; Voronezh Infantry, and 31st and 47th Jägers.
              26th ——— — Ladoga, Poltava, Nizhnii-Novgorod, and Orel Infantry and 42nd Jägers.

* These regiments were under the Navy Department [Morskoe vedomstvo].

The Pernau and Kexholm Infantry regiments were part of the 2nd Division, the Reval – of the 3rd, the Bryansk – of the 6th, the Libau and 49th Jägers – of the 7th, the Estonia – of the 14th, the 48th Jägers – of the 17th, the Lithuania and Podolia – of the 21st, and the Aleksopol and Butyrskii – of the 24th (30).

27 January 1811– The Mushketerskii Grafa Arakcheeva polk was renamed the Grenaderskii Grafa Arakcheeva polk [Graf Arakcheev's Grenadier Regiment] (31).

31 January 1811– Of the Replacement Recruit Depots established in 1809, the Nizhnii-Novgorod was abolished, and eight others were transferred to other places: the Zaslavl – to Beloi, the Ivenets – to Vyazma, the Vladimir – toYelna, the Dmitrovsk – to Romny, the Rovno – to Izyum, the Belgorod – to Bakhmut, the Tetyushi – to Taganrog, and the Chudnov – to Chigrin [Chigirin] (32).

3 February 1811–The Kavkazskii Grenaderskii polk was renamed the Gruzinskii Grenaderskii polk [Georgia Grenadier Regiment] (33).

7 February 1811–The Bryansk Replacement Recruit Depot was transferred to Starodub, and the Glukhov Depot to Konotop (34).

9 February 1811– The Rylsk, Yekaterinburg, and Selenginsk Infantry Regiments and the 18th Jägers were ordered to form the 23rd Division (35).

[22 February 1811 – All musketeer regiments were renamed infantry [pekhotnyi] regiments. - M.C.]

12 March 1811– Replacement Recruit Depots [Zapasnyya Rekrutskiya Depo] were ordered to be called simply Recruit Depots [Rekrutskiya Depo] (36).

12 March 1811– The 49-i Yegerskii polk was renamed the Sofiiskii Pekhotnyi polk [Sofiya Infantry Regiment] (37).

16 March 1811– Recruit Depots, except for the one at Yaroslavl which was left pending special instructions, were directed to be considered as belonging to divisions: the Roslavl Depot – to the 2nd Division, the Vyazma – to the 3rd, the Toropets – to the 4th, the Kholm – to the 5th, the Kargopol – to the 6th, the Starodub – to the 7th, the Novomirgorod – to the 8th, the Bakhmut – to the 9th, the Yelisavetgrad – to the 10th, the Izyum – to the 11th, the Akhtyrka – to the 12th, the Ivanovo – to the 13th, the Staraya-Russa – to the 14th, the Zmiev (transferred from Kharkov) – to the 15th, the Olviopol – to the 16th, the Belev – to the 17th, the Konotop – to the 18th, the Taganrog – to the 19th, the Azov – to the 20th, the Olonets – to the 21st, the Chigrin – to the 22nd, the Yelna – to the 23rd, the Novgorod-Severski – to the 24th, the Podgoshcha (transferred from Korostin [sic, Korosten]) – to the 25th, and the Romny – to the 26th. The 1st Division did not have a Recruit Depot (38).

27 March 1811– The Moscow and Kiev grenadier regiments were transferred to the 9th Division, and from the latter, to replace them, came infantry regiments: to the 8th Division – the Ukraine, to the 10th – the Bialystok (39).

27 March 1811– The 2nd Division was reformed anew, from Grenadier regiments: the Kiev, Astrakhan, Moscow, Phanagoria, Siberia, and Little Russia; the former 2nd Division was renamed the 11th; and the following regiments were reassigned from certain divisions to others: the Vladimir Infantry – from the 7th Division to the 18th; the Apsheron and Nasheburg Infantry – from the 11th to the 9th; the 11th Jägers – from the 11th to the 7th; the 40th Jägers – from the 11th to the 24th; the Yakutsk – from the 18th to the 9th; and the Aleksopol Infantry – from the 24th to the 18th (40).

7 July 1811– From the 19th and 20th Divisions, deployed in Georgia [Gruziya], there was formed the Georgia Corps [Gruzinskii Korpus] (41).

10 September 1811– In Petrozavodsk, Novgorod, Tver, Moscow, Kaluga, Orel, Kursk, Kharkov, and Yekaterinoslavl were established Recruit Depots of the 2nd Line [Rekrutskiya Depo 2-i linii], while the previously existing ones comprised the Recruit Depots of the 1st Line and were divided into divisions and brigades:

1st Division: 1st Brigade: Kargopol (16th Division) and Olonets (21st).
            2nd —— Podgoshcha (25th), Staraya-Russa (14th), and Kholm (5th).
            3rd —— Toropets (4th), Belev (17th), and Vyazma (3rd).
            4th —— Yelna (23rd) and Roslavl (11th).
2nd Division: 1st Brigade: Starodub (7th) and Novgorod-Severski (24th).
            2nd —— Konotop (18th), Romny (26th), and Akhtyrka (12th).
            3rd —— Zmiev (15th) and Izyum (9th).
            4th —— Chigrin (22nd), Novomirgorod (8th), Yelisavetgrad (10th), and Olviopol (16th).

Separate brigade under the command of the Military Governor of New Russia: Ivanovo (13th), Taganrog (19th), and Azov (20th) (42).

6 November 1811– New regiments were established: the Odesskii [Odessa],Vilenskii [Vilna], Tarnopolskii [Tarnopol],and Simbirskii [Simbirsk] Pekhotnye [Infantry], and the49-i and 50-i Yegerskie [Jägers], which formed the 27-ya diviziya (41).

Thus all the Grenadier, Infantry, and Jäger regiments formed twenty-seven divisions, in the following order.

1st Division   1st Brigade: Life-Grenadiers and Graf Arakcheev's Grenadiers (both with the Guards).
            2nd —— Pavlovsk and Yekaterinoslavl Grenadiers.
            3rd —— St.-Petersburg and Taurica Grenadiers.
2nd ——   1st —— Kiev and Moscow Grenadiers.
            2nd —— Astrakhan and Phanagoria Grenadiers.
            3rd —— Siberia and Little Russia Grenadiers.

3rd —— 1st —— Reval and Murom Infantry.
2nd —— Kopore and Chernigov.
3rd —— 20th and 21st Jägers.

4th —— 1st —— Kremenchug and Minsk Infantry.
2nd —— Tobolsk and Volhynia.
3rd —— 4th and 34th Jägers.

5th —— 1st —— Sevsk and Kaluga Infantry.
2nd —— Perm and Mogilev.
3rd —— 23rd and 24th Jägers.

6th —— 1st —— Bryansk and Nizovsk Infantry.
2nd —— Uglich Infantry and 35th Jägers.
3rd —— Azov Infantry and 3rd Jägers.

7th —— 1st —— Pskov and Mogilev Infantry.
2nd —— Libau and Sofiya Infantry.
3rd —— 36th and 11th Jägers.

8th —— 1st —— Ukraine and Archangel Infantry.
2nd —— Schlüsselburg and Old Ingermanland.
3rd —— 7th and 37th Jägers.

9th —— 1st —— Nasheburg and Yakutsk Infantry.
2nd —— Apsheron and Ryazhsk.
3rd —— 10th and 38th Jägers.

10th —— 1st —— Bialystok and Crimea Infantry.
2nd —— Kursk and Yaroslavl Infantry.
3rd —— 8th and 39th Jägers.

11th —— 1st —— Kexholm (with the Guards) and Pernau Infantry.
2nd —— Polotsk and Yelets.
3rd —— 1st and 33rd Jägers.

12th —— 1st —— Smolensk and Narva Infantry.
2nd —— Aleksopol and New Ingermanland.
3rd —— 6th and 41st Jägers.

13th —— 1st —— Galich and Velikie-Luki Infantry.
2nd —— Penza and Saratov.
3rd —— 12th and 22nd Jägers.

14th —— 1st —— Tula and Navaginsk Infantry.
2nd —— Estonia and Tenginsk.
3rd —— 25th and 26th Jägers.

15th —— 1st —— Kozlov and Vitebsk Infantry.
2nd —— Kura and Kolyvan.
3rd —— 13th and 14th Jägers.

16th —— 1st —— Okhotsk and Nyslott Infantry.
2nd —— Kamchatka and Mingrelia.
3rd —— 27th and 43rd Jägers.

17th —— 1st —— Ryazan and Belozersk Infantry.
2nd —— Villmanstrand and Brest.
3rd —— 30th and 48th Jägers.

18th —— 1st —— Vladimir and Tambov Infantry.
2nd —— Kostroma and Dnieper.
3rd —— 28th and 32nd Jägers.

21st —— 1st——Petrovsk and Podolia Infantry.
2nd——Neva and Lithuania.
3rd——2nd and 44th Jägers.

22nd —— 1st —— Vyatka and Staryi-Oskol Infantry.
2nd —— Olonets and Viborg.
3rd —— 29th and 45th Jägers.

23rd —— 1st —— Rylsk and Yekaterinburg Infantry.
2nd —— Selenginsk Infantry and 18th Jägers.

24th —— 1st —— Ufa and Shirvan Infantry.
2nd —— Butyrskii and Tomsk.

	3rd ——	40th and 19th Jägers.
25th ——	1st ——	1st and 2nd Marines.
	2nd ——	3rd Marines and Voronezh Infantry.
	3rd ——	31st and 47th Jägers.
26th ——	1st ——	Ladoga and Poltava Infantry.
	2nd ——	Nizhnii-Novgorod and Orel.
	3rd ——	5th and 42nd Jägers.
27th ——	1st ——	Odessa and Tarnopol Infantry.
	2nd ——	Vilna and Simbirsk.
	3rd ——	49th and 50th Jägers.

The 19th and 20th Divisions formed the Georgia Corps and comprised the regiments: 19th – Kazan, Suzdal, Belev, Sevastopol, Vologda, and 17th Jägers, and 20th – Caucasus and Kherson Grenadiers; Troitsk, Tiflis, and Kabarda Infantry, and 9th, 15th, and 46th Jägers, having no fixed or permanent distribution into brigades.

The 28th and 29th Divisions were composed of Garrison regiments and battalions in the Orenburg and Siberia territories (44).

19 November 1811– The Podgoshcha, Staraya-Russa, Kholm, Toropets, Belev, Vyazma, Starodub, Novgorod-Severski, Konotop, Romny, Akhtyrka, Zmiev, and Izyum Recruit Depots were ordered to be composed of six three-company battalions, the Roslavl – of five, and the Yelna – of four. These battalions were singly assigned to each of the infantry regiments of the 25th, 14th, 5th, 4th, 17th, 3rd, 7th, 24th, 18th, 26th, 12th, 15th, 9th, 11th, and 23rd Divisions and took up the name of fourth battalions of the regiments, also being called their Reserve [Rezervnyi] and Recruit [Rekrutskii] battalions (45).

22 November 1811– The Kargopol, Olonets, Belev, Chigrin, Novomirgorod, Yelisavetgrad, Olviopol, Ivanovo, Taganrog, and Azov depots, belonging to the 6th, 21st, 17th, 22nd, 8th, 10th, 16th, 13th, 19th, and 20th Divisions, were ordered to each have six three-company battalions, which received the name of fourth Rezervnye [chetvertye Rezervnye] or Recruit [Rekrutskie] battalions of those regiments to which they were assigned, and at this time all Recruit Depots belonged to divisions as follows: Vyazma – 3rd, Toropets – 4th, Kholm – 5th, Kargopol – 6th, Starodub – 7th, Novomirgorod – 8th, Izyum – 9th, Yelisavetgrad – 10th, Roslavl – 11th, Akhtyrka – 12th, Ivanovo – 13th, Staraya-Russa – 14th, Zmiev – 15th, Olviopol – 16th, Belev – 17th, Konotop – 18th, Taganrog – 19th, Azov – 20th, Olonets – 21st, Chigrin – 22nd, Yelna – 23rd, Novgorod-Severski – 24th, Podgoshcha – 25th, and Romny – 26th. Thus, only two Depots were not divided into battalions: the Yaroslavl and Bakhmut; and in the Army infantry only Grenadier regiments did not have fourth battalions. Along with these orders, the 1st and 2nd Reserve Divisions, composed of Reserve battalions, were called the 1st and 2nd Reserve Corps [1-i i 2-i Rezervnye Korpusa], and Reserve brigades were renamed Reserve divisions [Rezervnyya divizii] (46).

14 March 1812– It was ordered to form 18 new Infantry divisions from the second or Replacement [Zapasnyi] battalions (without Grenadier companies) and fourth or Reserve [Rezervnyi] battalions:

30th — from the Replacement btns: of the 14th Division: Tula, Navginsk, Tenginsk, and Estonia Infantry, and 25th and 26th Jägers, and of the 4th Division: Kremenchug, Volhynia, Tobolsk, and Minsk Infantry, and 4th and 34th Jägers.

31st of the 5th Division: Sevsk, Kaluga, Perm, and Mogilev Infantry, and 23rd and 24th Jägers, and of the 17th Division: Ryazan, Brest, Villmanstrand, and Belozersk Infantry, and 30th and 48th Jägers.

32nd of the 1st Division: St.-Petersburg, Yekaterinoslavl, Pavlovsk, and Taurica Grenadiers; of the 23rd Division:Rylsk, Yekaterinburg, and Selenginsk Infantry, and 18th Jägers, and of the 11th Division:Polotsk and Pernau Infantry and 1st and 33rd Jägers.

33rd of the 3rd Division: Reval, Murom, Kopore, and Chernigov Infantry, and 20th and 21st Jägers, and of the 7th Division: Pskov, Moscow, Libau, and Sofiya Infantry, and 36th and 11th Jägers.

34th of the 24th Division: Ufa, Shirvan, Butyrskii, and Tomsk Infantry, and 40th and 19th Jägers, and of the 26th Division: Ladoga, Poltava, Nizhnii-Novgorod, and Orel Infantry, and 5th and 24th Jägers.

35th of the 2nd Division: Kiev, Moscow, Astrakhan, Phanagoria, Siberia, and Little Russia Grenadiers, and of the 18th Division: Vladimir, Tambov, Kostroma, and Dnieper Infantry, and 28th and 32nd Jägers.

36th of the 12th Division: Smolensk, Narva, Aleksopol, and New Ingermanland Inf., and 6th and 41st Jägers, and of the 15th Division: Kozlov, Vitebsk, Kura, and Kolyvan Infantry, and 13th and 14th Jägers.

37th of the 27th Division: Odessa, Tarnopol, Vilna, and Simbirsk Infantry, and 49th and 50th Jägers, and of the 9th Division: Nasheburg, Yakutsk, Apsheron, and Ryazhsk Infantry, and 10th and 38th Jägers.

38th of the Kargopol Depot, i.e. 6th Division: Bryansk, Nizovsk, Uglich, and Azov Infantry, and 35th and 3rd Jägers, and of the Olonets Depot, i.e. 21st Division: Petrovsk, Podolia, Neva, and Lithuania Infantry, and 2nd and 42nd Jägers.

39th of the Podgoshcha Depot, i.e. 25th Division: 1st, 2nd, and 3rd Marines, Voronezh Infantry, and 31st and 47th Jägers, and of the Staraya-Russa Depot, i.e. 14th Division: Tula, Navaginsk, Estonia and Tenginsk Infantry, and 25th and 26th Jägers.

40th of the Kholm Depot, i.e. 5th Division: Sevsk, Kaluga, Perm, and Mogilev Inf., and 23rd and 24th Jägers, and of the Toropets Depot, i.e. 4th Division: Kremenchug, Minsk, Tobolsk, and Volhynia Infantry, and 4th and 34th Jägers.

41st of the Belev Depot, i.e. 17th Division: Ryazan, Belozersk, Villmanstrand, and Brest Infantry, and 30th and 48th Jägers, and of the Vyazma Depot, i.e. 3rd Division: Reval, Murom, Kopore, and Chernigov Infantry, and 20th and 21st Jägers.

42nd of the Yelna Depot, i.e. 23rd Division: Rylsk, Yekaterinburg, and Selenginsk Infantry, and 18th Jägers; of the Roslavl Depot, i.e. 11th Division: Kexholm, Pernau, and Polotsk Inf., and 1st and 33rd Jägers, and of the Starodub Depot,i.e. 7th Division:Pskov, Moscow, Libau, and Sofiya Infantry, and 36th and 11th Jägers.

43rd of the Novgorod-Severskii Depot, i.e. 24th Division: Ufa, Shirvan, Butyrskii, and Tomsk Infantry, and 40th and 19th Jägers, and of the Konotop Depot, i.e. 18th Division: Vladimir, Tobolsk, Kostroma, and Dnieper Infantry, and 28th and 32nd Jägers.

44th of the Romny Depot, i.e. 26th Division: Ladoga, Poltava, Nizhnii-Novgorod, and Orel Infantry, and 5th and 42nd Jägers, and of the Akhtyrka Depot, i.e. 12th Division: Smolensk, Narva, Aleksopol, and New Ingermanland Infantry, and 6th and 41st Jägers.

45th of the Zmiev Depot, i.e. 15th Division: Kozlov, Vilna, Kura, and Kolyvan Infantry, and 13th and 14th Jägers, and of the Izyum Depot, i.e. 9th Division: Nasheburg, Yakutsk, Apsheron, and Ryazhsk Infantry, and 10th and 38th Jägers.

46th of the Chigrin Depot, i.e. 22nd Division: Vyatka, Staryi-Oskol, Olonets, and Viborg Infantry, and 29th and 45th Jägers, and of the Novomirgorod Depot, i.e. 8th Division: Ukraine, Archangel, Schlüsselburg, and Old Ingermanland Infantry, and 7th and 37th Jägers.

47th of the Yelisavetgrad Depot, i.e. 10th Division: Bialystok, Crimea, Kursk, and Yaroslavl Infantry, and 8th and 39th Jägers, and of the Olviopol Depot, i.e. 16th Division: Okhotsk, Nyslott, Kamchatka, and Mingrelia Infantry, and 27th and 43rd Jägers.

The Life-Grenadiers (of the 1st Division), Graf Arakcheev's Grenadiers (1st Division), and the Kexholm Infantry (11th Division), being with the Guards troops, did not detach their second battalions, while the first of these, as all Grenadier regiments, did not have a Reserve battalion. The second and Reserve battalions of the Yelets Regiment (11th Division) were located on their settlement in Mogilev Province, and therefore were not part of the Reserve forces; likewise second battalions were not detached from the 19th and 20th Divisions stationed in Georgia and the Caucasus, and whose Reserve battalions were soon disbanded.

Combined Grenadier Battalions[Svodnye Grenaderskie bataliony] were formed from the Grenadier companies of second battalions, based on the regulation of 22 October, 1811, set forth above:

With the 1st Division:
1st Battalion from the companies of: the Yekaterinoslavl, St.-Petersburg, and Pavlovsk Grenadier regiments.
2nd ——— —— —————— — Graf Arakcheev's Grenadiers and the Kexholm Infantry. [The Taurica Grenadiers are omitted. An error? — M.C.]

With the 2nd Division:
1st Battalion from the companies of: the Moscow, Kiev, and Astrakhan Grenadiers.
2nd ——— —— —————— — the Phanagoria, Little Russia, and Siberia Grenadiers.

With the 3rd Division:
1st Battalion from the companies of: the Chernigov, Kopore, and 21st Jägers.
2nd ——— —— —————— — the Reval, Murom, and 20th Jägers.

With the 4th Division:
1st Battalion from the companies of: the Kremenchug, Lithuania [sic, Minsk], and 4th Jägers.
2nd ——— —— —————— — the Tobolsk, Volhynia, and 34th Jägers.

With the 5th Division:
1st Battalion from the companies of: the Sevsk, Kaluga, and 23rd Jägers.
2nd ——— —— —————— — the Perm, Mogilev, and 24th Jägers.

With the 6th Division:
1st Battalion from the companies of: the Bryansk, Nizovsk, and 35th Jägers.
2nd ——— —— —————— — the Uglich, Azov, and 3rd Jägers.

With the 7th Division:
1st Battalion from the companies of: the Pskov, Moscow, and 36th Jägers.
2nd ——— —— —————— — the Libau, Sofiya, and 11th Jägers.

With the 9th Division:
1st Battalion from the companies of: the Nasheburg, Yakutsk, and 10th Jägers.
2nd ——— —— —————— — the Apsheron, Ryazhsk, and 38th Jägers.

With the 11th Division:
1st Battalion from the companies of: the Pernau and 1st Jägers.
2nd ——— —— —————— — the Polotsk and 33rd Jägers.

With the 12th Division:
1st Battalion from the companies of: the Smolensk, Narva, and 6th Jägers.
2nd ——— —— —————— — the Aleksopol, New Ingermanland, and 41st Jägers.

With the 14th Division:

1st Battalion from the companies of: the Navaginsk, Estonia, and 26th Jägers.

2nd ——— —— ————— — the Tula, Tenginsk, and 25th Jägers.

> With the 15th Division:

1st Battalion from the companies of: the Kozlov, Vitebsk, and 13th Jägers.

2nd ——— —— ————— — the Kursk, Kolyvan, and 14th Jägers.

> With the 17th Division:

1st Battalion from the companies of: the Ryazan, Belozersk, and 30th Jägers.

2nd ——— —— ————— — the Brest, Villmanstrand, and 48th Jägers.

> With the 18th Division:

1st Battalion from the companies of: the Vladimir, Tambov, and 28th Jägers.

2nd ——— —— ————— — the Kostroma, Dnieper, and 32nd Jägers.

> With the 23rd Division:

1st Battalion from the companies of: the Rylsk and Yekaterinburg.

2nd ——— —— ————— — the Selenginsk and 18th Jägers.

> With the 24th Division:

1st Battalion from the companies of: the Ufa, Shirvan, and 40th Jägers.

2nd ——— —— ————— — the Butyrskii, Tomsk, and 19th Jägers.

> With the 26th Division:

1st Battalion from the companies of: the Ladoga, Poltava, and 5th Jägers.

2nd ——— —— ————— — the Nizhnii-Novgorod, Orel, and 42nd Jägers.

> With the 27th Division:

1st Battalion from the companies of: the Odessa, Tarnopol, and 49th Jägers.

2nd ——— —— ————— — the Vilna, Simbirsk, and 50th Jägers.

The 6th, 21st, and 25th Divisions, quartered in Finland; the 8th, 10th, 13th, 16th, and 22nd, on campaign against the Turks; and the 19th and 20th, stationed in Georgia and the Caucasus—did not have Combined Grenadier battalions (47).

15 March 1812– The Infantry divisions formed from Zapasnyi and Rezervnyi battalions were assigned to the newly established Reserve armies [Rezervnyya armii], but since war with France soon broke out these armies were not completely formed:

> 32nd, 33rd, 39th, 40th, 41st, and 42nd Divisions — to the 1st Reserve Army;
> 34th, 35th, 36th, and 37th Divisions — to the 2nd Reserve Army;
> 43rd, 44th, 45th, 46th, and 47th Divisions — to the 3rd Reserve, Observation, Army.

The 30th and 31st Divisions were not assigned to these armies, but formed the garrison in the city of Riga, and the 38th was used to fill out various regiments (48).

19 March 1812– With the organization of the 1st and 2nd Western Armies [1-ya i 2-ya Zapadnyya armii] from the forces deployed on the Empire's western border, the first comprised: the 1st, 3rd, 4th, 5th, 7th, 11th, 14th, 17th, 23rd, and 24th Infantry Divisions, and the second: the 2nd, 12th, 26th, and 27th. All were with their Combined Grenadier battalions (49).

1 May 1812– From the recruits mustered in Yaroslavl, Vladimir, Kostroma, Voronezh, Ryazan, and Tambov were established new regiments: 1st, 2nd, 3rd, 4th, 5th, 6th, 7th, and 8th Infantry, and 1st, 2nd, 3rd, and 4th Jägers (50).

5 May 1812– With the formation of the new 3rd Reserve Observation Army [3-ya Rezervnaya Observatsionnaya armiya] (in place of the one never organized), it was assigned the following Infantry divisions: 9th, 15th, and 18th, with their Combined Grenadier battalions, as well as the Zapasnyi battalions of the 15th and 18th Divisions. Additionally, as related above, the 8th, 10th, 13th, 16th, and 22nd Divisions were in the Danube Army [Dunaiskaya armiya]; the 6th, 21st, and 25th – in Finland; and the 19th and 20th – in Georgia and on the Caucasian Line.

The Zapasnyi and Rezervnyi battalions enumerated above were in part distributed to the various corps, where they subsequently were used to replace losses in personnel, and in part, at the very beginning of military operations, used to bring the forces up to strength under the direct orders of the Commanders-in-Chief of the armies.

By the month of June, i.e. by the time the forces of the Emperor Napoleon crossed over the Russian borders, the distribution of Infantry divisions to the three armies facing him was as follows:

a.) In the 1st Western Army [1-ya Zapadnaya armiya]:

In the 1st Inf. Corps — 5th and 4th Divisions, with their Combined Grenadier Battalions and the Zapasnyi battalions of the 1st, 3rd, 4th, 7th, 11th, and 23rd Divisions.

> —— 2nd - 4th and 17th Divisions, with their Combined Grenadier Battalions.
> —— 3rd - 1st and 3rd Divisions, with their Combined Grenadier Battalions.
> —— 4th - 11th and 23rd Divisions, with their Combined Grenadier Battalions.
> —— 6th - 7th and 24th Divisions, with their Combined Grenadier Battalions.

b.) In the 2nd Western Army [2-ya Zapadnaya armiya]:

In the 7th Inf. Corps — 26th and 12th Divisions.

8th 2nd Division and Combined Grenadier Division from the second Grenadier companies of the 2nd, 26th, and 12th Divisions.

c.) In the 3rd Reserve Observation Army [3-ya Rezervnaya Observatsionnaya armiya]:

In Lt.-Gen. Morkov's Corps — 9th and 15th Divisions.

— Graf Kamenskii's ——— — 18th Division and the Combined Grenadier Battalions of the 9th, 15th, and 18th Divisions.

— Lt.-Gen. Saken's ——— — 36th Division, composed of the Zapasnyi battalions of the 12th and 15th Divisions (51).

27 June 1812– From recruits of the Recruit Depots of the 2nd Line were established: the 9-i, 10-i, 11-i, 12-i, 13-i, and 14-i Pekhotnye polki [Infantry regiments], and afterwards all Recruit Depots were disbanded (52).

16 September 1812– The 1-ya and 2-ya Zapadnyya armii [1st and 2nd Western Armies] were combined into one, under the name Glavnaya armiya [Main Army] (53).

17 September 1812– From the 3-ya Rezervnaya Observatsionaya armiya [3rd Reserve Observation Army] and the Dunaiskaya armiya [Danube Army] was formed the 3-ya Zapadnaya armiya [3rd Western Army] (54).

26 October 1812– Having been established in May and June of this year, the 1st, 2nd, 3rd, 4th, 5th, 6th, 7th, 8th, 9th, 10th, 11th, 12th, 13th, and 14th Infantry regiments and the 1st, 2nd, 3rd, and 4th Jäger regiments were disbanded in order to provide replacements for the other forces in the Main Army (55).

After this, during the remaining months of 1812, in 1813, and in the greater half of 1814, there were many changes in the composition and names themselves of the armies, corps, and divisions operating against the enemy, directly resulting from the course of the war. Being only temporary measures on the part of the Commanders-in-Chief, they belong more to a history of the military operations of that time then to a survey of the basic changes in the composition and nomenclature of the forces, and therefore only those Government orders will be presented below which directed changes that were not just applicable to wartime.

NOTES

(1) Highest Order.

(2) Highest Order.

(3) Complete Collection of Laws of the Russian Empire [Polnoe Sobranie Zakonov Rossiiskoi Imperii, hereafter PSZ], Vol. XXVI, pg. 723, No. 19,951.

(4) Highestconfirmed Personnel Tables [Shtaty] for Grenadier, Musketeer, and Jäger regiments, 30 April, 1802.

(5) PSZ, Vol. XXVII, pg. 412, No. 20,569.

(6) Highest Order and PSZ, Vol. XLIII, part II, pg. 14, No. 20,674, and Vol. XXVII, pg. 604, № 20,764.

(7) Highest Order and PSZ, Vol. XXVIII, pg. 1,186, No. 21,882, and Vol. XLIII, part II, sect. I, pg. 38, No. 21,928.

(8) Highest Order and PSZ, Vol. XXVIII, pg. 1,284, No. 21,942.

(9) Report of General-Adjutant Graf Liven to His Imperial Highness the Tsesarevich Constantine Pavlovich, from 4 May, 1806, № 1,307.

(10) PSZ, Vol. XXIX, pg. 368, No. 22,174.

(11) PSZ, Vol. XXIX, pg. 571, No. 22,176.

(12) Highest Order; PSZ, Vol. XXIX, pg. 693, No. 22,245; and Army List for 1806.

(13) Army List for 1807.

(14) Ibid.

(15) Ibid.

(16) PSZ, Vol. XXX, pg. 58, No. No. 22,807 and 22,808.

(17) Highest Order and Army List for 1808.

(18) Highest Order.

(19) PSZ, Vol. XXX, pp. 603 and 637, No. 23,297.

(20) List of Replacement Recruit Depots, for 1809.

(21) PSZ, Vol. XXX, pg. 901, No. 23,565.

(22) PSZ, Vol. XXX, pg. 1,070, No. 23,787.

(23) Army List for 1809, and PSZ, Vol. XLIV, part II, Regulations on Uniforms, pg. 68, No. 23,949.

(24) PSZ, Vol. XXXI, pg. 420, No. 24,400.

(25) Highest Order.

(26) PSZ, Vol. XXXI, pg. 395, No. 24,386.

(27) PSZ, Vol. XXXI, pg. 466, No. 24,446.
(28) Highest Order.
(29) Archive of the Department of Military Settlements, report on the activities of the Settled battalion of the Yelets Infantry Regiment, Book 7, pg. 362.
(30) Highest Order.
(31) Signed Order to the Military College, 27 January, 1811.
(32) PSZ, Vol. XXXI, pg. 531, No. 24,504.
(33) Highest Order.
(34) PSZ, Vol. XXXI, pg. 545, No. 24,514.
(35) Highest Order.
(36) PSZ, Vol. XXXI, pg. 577, No. 24,553.
(37) PSZ, Vol. XXXI, pg. 577, No. 24,554.
(38) PSZ, Vol. XXXI, pg. 582, No. 24,559.
(39) PSZ, Vol. XXXI, pg. 593, No. 24,567.
(40) PSZ, Vol. XXXI, pg. 598, No. 24,569.
(41) PSZ, Vol. XXXI, pg. 810, No. 24,715.
(42) PSZ, Vol. XXXI, pp. 835 and 836, No. 24,764, and Vol. XLIII, part II, sect. 1, pg. 359, No. 24,762.
(43) Highest Order addressed to the Minister of War, from 6 November, 1811.
(44) Archive of the Inspection Department [Inspektorskii Departament] of the Ministry of War, Book of Orders of the Military College, under No. 40, sheet 133.
(45) Orders of the Military College, for 1811.
(46) PSZ, Vol. XXXI, pg. 909, No. 24,889.
(47) PSZ, Vol. XXXII, pg. 231, No. 25,039, and List of forces for 1812.
(48) Highest Order and List of forces for 1812.
(49) Description of the Patriotic War, in 1812, by G. L. Mikhailovskii-Danilevskii, St. Petersburg, 1839. Part I, pg. 128.
(50) PSZ, Vol. XXXII, pg. 305, No. 25,099.
(51) List of forces for 1812, in the St.-Petersburg and Moscow Archives of the Inspection Department of the Ministry of War.
(52) PSZ, Vol. XXXII, pg. 375, No. 25,166.
(53) Order of General-Field Marshal Prince Kutuzov, from 16 September, 1812.
(54) Description of the Patriotic War, in 1812, by G. L. Mikhailovskii-Danilevskii, St. Petersburg, 1839. Part III, pg. 216, and Army List for 1812.
(55) Proposal by Prince Gorchakov, Director of the Departments of the Ministry of War, to the Inspection Department.

Russian troops under Suvorov crossing the Alps in 1799. The first "Napoleonic" Russian clash

Russian Army: Grenadiers, 1801-1825

I. GRENADIER REGIMENTS

9 April 1801— Lower ranks are ordered to cut off their **curls** [*pukli*] and have **queues** [*kosy*] only 7 inches long, tying them midway down the collar (665).

[**14 April 1801**— All infantry and Artillery regiments are to wear black neckclothes, but lower ranks are not to begin before the wear-out period of the old neckclothes (Highest Order). - M.C.]

24 June 1801— Generals and field and company-grade officers of the **St.-Petersburg garrison**, i.e. the troops located in St. Petersburg, including the Leib-Grenadier and Pavlovsk Grenadier regiments, are ordered to wear **hats** of the new pattern, the same as described below in the description of Grenadier uniforms according to the table of 30 April 1802 (666).

15 January 1802— New rules are confirmed regarding the cutting and sewing of uniforms for combatant and noncombatant, or lower-staff [*unter-shtabnye*] personel (667).

17 March 1802— Supplementary regulations are confirmed regarding the pattern for **coats**, by which, among other things, it is ordered that: in all regiments which have Princes of the Blood [*Printsy Krovi*] as Honorary Colonels [*Shefi*], officer's coats are to have gold or silver (according to the color of the buttons) **embroidered buttonholes** [*petlitsy*]; on each side of the collar - two, and on the cuffs - according to the number of buttons. Additionally, for officers and combatant lower ranks of the **Leib-Grenadiers aiguillettes** [*akselbanty*] are kept as before, on the right shoulder: for the first - gold, and for the latter - of yellow worsted [*garus*] (668).

30 April 1802— Confirmation is given to the **new table of uniforms**, accouterments, and weapons of Grenadier regiments. Based upon this table, as well as on the four directives presented above, *privates* [*ryadovye*] of the the first, or Honorary Colonels' [*Shefskie*], *Grenadier battalions* are prescribed: *coat* [*mundir*] or *caftan* [*kaftan*], *pants* [*pantalony*]; *boots* [*sapogi*]; *neckcloth* [*galstuk*]; *forage* and *grenadier caps* [*furazhnaya i grenaderskaya shapki*]; *greatcoat* [*shinel*], *warm coat* [*fufaika*]; *sword* [*shpaga*] with *swordknot* [*temlyak*]; *swordbelt* [*portupeya*], *musket* [*ruzhe*] with *bayonet* [*shtyk*], *sling* [*remen*], *lock cover* [*ognivnyi chekhol*] and *frizzen protector* [*polunagalishche*]; *cartridge pouch* [*patronnaya suma*] with *crossbelt* [*perevyaz*]; *knapsack* [*ranets*], and *water flask* [*vodonosnaya flyazha*]. The coat was to be double-breasted, of dark-green cloth, with a standing collar of a special color for each Inspectorate; with cuffs the same color as the collar; with dark-green flaps on the cuffs; with red kersey lining, with brass buttons and two shoulder straps [*pogony*], of a special color for each regiment in an Inspectorate. The lower edge or lining of the collar and shoulder straps were dark green (Illus. 1274). This coat was to have all buttons fastened in summer as well as winter, and the sizes of its parts, assuming a man of 6 feet in height, were prescribed to be as follows:

Collar height, in front, at the edges - 3 1/2 inches, behind, at the middle - 4 3/8 inches; the upper edge shorter than the lower by 3 1/2 inches.

Length of the caftan, from the collar to the waist - 17 1/2 inches, and from the waist to the end of the tails - 15 3/4 inches; width of the turnover - 3 inches; the distance of the first button from the collar - 7/8 inch; between the first and second buttons and so on - 2 5/8 inches; between the buttonholes and the edge of the turnover - 7/8 inch.

Turnbacks on the tails, along the straight edge - 17 inches, along the other edge - 14 7/8 inches, on the upper edge - 1 1/3 inches; width below - 4 7/8 inches.

Width of the cuffs - 3 inches, and of the flap - 1 3/4 inches; length of the flap - 6 1/8 inches.

Length of the shoulder strap - 5 3/4 inches; its width at the shoulder - 1 3/4 inches, width at the button - 1 1/4 inches.

Buttons were flat, 25 in number, namely: on the right side of the turnover - 7; on the left - 6; on the cuffs opposite the buttonholes - 2 each; on the upper buttonhole of the flaps - 1 each; at the lower edge of the collar, for the shoulder straps - 2; on the waist - 2; at the joining of the turnbacks on the tails - 1 each (Illus. 1274).

Pants, of white wool cloth but in summer of Flemish linen - 37 5/8 inches long from the edge of the swordbelt, i.e. reaching to within 8 3/4 inches of the heels, and having a panel [*latsbant*] in front of such a width that it is covered by the coat skirts. In front under the panel, and behind on the waist hem, 1 3/4 inches from the top edge of the pants, were sewn two covered buttons each, for suspenders [*pomochi*], arranged so that they could be fastened and unfastened easily without removing the swordbelt.

Boots, polished, with round toes - 14 inches high from the heels, i.e. 5 1/4 inches above the lower edge of the pants - made with a 1 3/4 inch cut-out in back and 7/8-inch heels. There were also small leather ears with buttonholes sewn inside the tops of the boots, which fastened to small leather buttons fixed to the side seams of the pants

Neckcloth, with a small dicky, made from black cloth on a linen lining and fastened behind by four small ribbons. Its height and width were not fixed, and there was only a rule in regard to the dicky which said that if a man had loosened the top button of his coat then the dicky was not to be visible when he raised his head up.

Forage cap- of dark-green cloth, with a band the same color as the collar or with no band at all, and with piping on the seams the same color as the shoulder straps. It kept almost the same form as it had during the previous reign. Its height from the lower edge to where it bent over was prescribed to be 8 3/4 inches; the distance from where it bent over to the tassel and knot - 10 1/2 inches; width where it bent over - 10 1/2 inches; width at the knot at the end - 1 1/4 inches; tassel - 2 5/8 inches; width of the band - 3 1/2 inches (Illus. 1274). The tassel was to be of two colors: green and the color of the shoulder straps. The knot was according to the company: in the first companies of battalions - white, in the second - red, in the third - sky blue, and in the fourth - orange. In regard to the coiffure, care was taken that the front hair, or *laverzhet* as it was called then, and hair at the temples was cropped smooth and short, while the hair at the rear was tied into a thick, flat queue intertwined with a black, woolen ribbon so that the end of the hair protruded just a bit. Powder was only used at big parades and holidays.

Grenadier cap- of almost the same form and size as under Emperor Paul I, namely: with a brass plate in front; with three grenades - also of brass - behind and on the sides. On the first, i.e. the plate, there was almost over its entire height a raised image of the double-headed Russian eagle with St. George on the breast. The top part [*verkhushka*] was according the the color of the collar and cuffs, while the rear piece or band [*zadnik ili okolysh*] was according to the color of the shoulder straps. The edging around the plate and below the band was black, as before. The trim on the top part was white cotton tape, while the pompons were according to the special list located below (Illus. 1275).

Greatcoat- of undyed cloth, dark or light grey, only being the same shade for the whole regiment; with a collar and shoulder straps the same color and pattern as on the coat, and with round grey cuffs. It was made so that it not only could be worn over the coat, but additionally over the warm coat or half-length fur coat. In front it was fastened with seven flat brass buttons, sewn on with such a distance between one and the next that when the swordbelt was worn over the greatcoat, the very bottom button was under the swordbelt, while the top button of the rear flaps was over the swordbelt (Illus. 1276).

The *warm coat*, or half-length fur coat [*polushubok*], was of sheepskin as before.

Sword, with a cutlass-like [*tesachnyi*] blade, brass hilt [*yefes*], a similar brass hook and endpiece, and with a scabbard of unblackened leather. It was unchanged from before (Illus. 1277).

The *swordbelt* was, as before, of deerskin, whitened, and 2 inches wide; with an adjustable brass buckle; with two frogs [*lopasti*] for the sword and the bayonet scabbard, and with welts near the edges. At its front edge, the frog was prescribed to be 6 1/8 inches long from the swordbelt to the slit into which the sword was placed, and the distance along the lower edge of the swordbelt, between both ends of the frog and depending on the individual body size, was about 5 to 7 inches. As a rule, when the swordbelt was worn it had to be adjusted so that when the rear end of the frog was between both waist buttons and pulled flat against the left one of these, then the sword was not to project forward and the left hand of a man standing upright was to lie above and alongside the hilt. The lower edge of the swordbelt had to lie above and right next to the waist buttons (Illus. 1277).

The *swordknot* consisted of a strap, small loop [*gaechka*], acorn [*derevyashaka*], *trinchik*, or colored ring, and the fringe. The length of the strap was prescribed to be 19 3/4 inches long and its width 7/8 inch; the distance from the top of the loop to the colored ring was 1 3/4 inches, the colored ring was 1/2 inch; the fringe was 7/8 inch. The swordknot was tied to the sword with an opening or loop under the knob on the hilt and wrapped around the whole length of the guard, leaving the tassel free for 3 1/2 inches (Illus. 1277). For all privates the strap and fringe of the swordknot remained white cotton; acorns - the same color as the collar and cuffs, and the loops and color rings: in the 1st company - white, in the 2nd - red, in the 3rd - sky blue, and in the 4th - orange.

Musket, along with its sling, lock cover, and frizzen cover; cartridge pouch, with brass plate and four grenades also of brass, and crossbelt, 3 3/4 inches wide, with welts along the edges. All these remain as previously laid down in the table of 5 January 1798 (Illus. 1277).

Knapsack, of black, dried leather, lined with linen, made round, 15 3/4 inches long and 8 1/4 inches across, and having a cover 8 3/4 inches wide that was closed by three iron buckles and, over them, two leather buttons. Inside it was a divider of doubled linen for putting three days worth of rusk into one half, and in the other - baggage, as follows: two shirts, foot wraps, wool kerchiefs, half-length fur coat, summer or winter (depending on the time of year) pants, brush, polish, soap, chalk, etc. The knapsack was put on over the right shoulder with the help of a whitened, deerskin belt 1 1/8 inches wide, fastened by two iron buckles at the sides of the knapsack so that it lay close to the shoulders, somewhat at a slant, with the right side upward (Illus. 1277).

Waterflask, made from double thickness iron and keeping the previous shape and size, i.e. height, without the cap - 6 3/8 inches, with the cap - 7 7/8 inches, breadth - 6 1/2 inches, and width - 3 inches. It was strapped to middle of the knapsack with white deerskin straps 5/8 inch wide (Illus. 1277).

Noncommissioned officers [unter-ofitsery] of *Grenadier battalions* were uniformed the same as private grenadiers but with only one shoulder strap, on the right shoulder, and with the additional distinction that along the lower and side edges of the collar and along the upper edge of the cuffs they had gold galloon [galun], 5/8 inch wide. and the pompon on the grenadier cap and the trinchik or colored ring of the swordknot were white with black and orange mixed in. Also, as before, they wore white chamois gloves with rounded cuffs 2 5/8 inches wide and carried a cane stick [trost] with a knob made of white bone and a brass endpiece, of such a length that if a person holds it in his right hand under the knob and lets its end point to the toe of the right foot, it then would reach the floor. In formation, the stick, by means of a leather strap passed through it below the knob, hung on the right side from the second coat button from the top, and then was put through a double black leather strap, 5/8 inch wide, fastened to the right waist button. When out of formation, when the stick was held in the hand, this strap was unfastened and put away.

Of the six junior noncommissioned officers [mladshchie unter-ofitsery] in each company of a Grenadier battalion, four were to have rifled muskets and black leather front pouches [podsumki] with a brass plate and four grenades, also of brass. As it was under Emperor Paul I, the other two noncommissioned officers, as well as the supply sergeant [kaptenarmus] and first sergeant [feldfebel] kept the halberds [alebardy] of the previous pattern, whose hafts were specially colored according to the list appended below. Officer candidates [podpraporshchiki] and distinguished officer candidates [portupei-praporshchiki] did not have muskets or halberds, but just the stick (Illus. 1278). Noncommissioned officers had knapsacks like the privates but wore them across the left shoulder instead of the right.

Company drummers [rotnye barabanshchiki] of *Grenadier battalions* were uniformed the same as grenadiers but were distinguished from them by wings or shoulder pieces [kryltsy ili naplechniki] of dark-green cloth with white cotton tape 5/8 inch wide. This tape was sewn on along the round or bottom edges of the wings and along the side of the left coat edge, but in half width so that half of it was above and half underneath. Tape was on the wings - four rows in full width; on the upper halves of the sleeves - six rows in full width with points up; and on the left coat side of the coat and on the cuff flaps, opposite buttonholes and buttons, laid double in the shape of the buttonhole (Illus. 1279). The *drum* was prescribed to be of brass *without a badge*, with dark-green and white triangles painted on the hoops, ropes to tighten the frame or hoops, and white deerskin ears or looseners.

Drumsticks were according to the color of the flagstaffs and halberd shafts. The *crossbelt for the drum* was 4 3/8 inches wide, deerskin, whitened, with two holders of that same material for the drumsticks, a small strap to suspend the drum from, and without any metal appointments. An *apron* [zanaveska] for protecting the pants was of calfskin, made with the hair on the outside (Illus. 1279).

Fifers [fleishchiki] of *Grenadier battalions* were uniformed like company drummers of these battalions and kept their brass cases of the previous pattern to hold the fife, worn on a white deerskin belt (Illus. 1279).

Battalion drummers [batalionnye barabanshchiki] of *Grenadier battalions* differed from company drummers in that they had seven rows of tape sewn on their coat sleeves instead of six, and also in having this on all seams, on the edge of the left side of the coat, and on the tails along the turnbacks. Like noncommissioned officers, they had gold galloon on the collar and cuffs; the pompon of the grenadier cap and the trinchik of the swordknot were white with black and orange; they had gloves and a cane (Illus. 1280).

Privates of Fusilier battalions [ryadovye fuzelernykh batalionov], except for the cap worn in formation and the cartridge pouch, had entirely the same uniform, accouterments, and armaments as privates of Grenadier battalions. Their formation caps [stroevyya shapki], or *fusilier caps* [fuzelernyya shapki], had almost the same appearance as they had under Emperor Paul I, only a little taller, namely: 10 inches tall with the plate, this having exactly the same image on it as the plate for grenadier caps (Illus. 1281). And fusilier pouches had only the badge without the grenades in the corners (Illus. 1282).

Junior noncommissioned officers, supply sergeants, and sergeants [*mladshie unter-ofitsery, kaptenarmusy i feldfebeli*] of Fusilier battalions were uniformed and armed like these ranks in Grenadier battalions with only the grenadier cap being replaced by the fusilier cap described above, and with the additional difference that all without exception had *halberds*. Officer candidates and distinguished officer candidates were not prescribed these last items.

Company and battalion drummers of Fusilier battalions were uniformed and armed as in Grenadier battalions except the grenadier cap was replaced by the fusilier cap.

The regimental drummer and musicians [*polkovyi barabanshchik i muzykanty*] (two each for bassoons, waldhorns, clarinets, and fifes, and one for a drum) were uniformed and armed like battalion drummers in Grenadier battalions, without any difference.

Apart from the equipment and weapons described here, each Grenadier and Fusilier company was issued *entrenching tools* [*shantsovye instrumenty*]: 20 axes, 10 iron spades, and 5 picks and mattocks [5 of each? — M.C.], with covers made from worn-out pouches and with 1 1/2 inch straps for them made from similarly worn-out crossbelts and swordbelts. The ax handle was prescribed to be 2 feet 5 inches long; the length of the spade handle - exactly 2 feet 4 inches; the width of the ax cover: top - 10 inches, bottom - 10 1/2 inches; its length - 9 1/8 inches; width of the spade cover - 9 1/8 inches; its length - 11 3/8 inches.

Company-grade officers [*ober-ofitsery*] *of Grenadier regiments* had a coat, pants, and boots of the same colors and patterns as prescribed for private grenadiers, except that the first did not have a seventh button under the right side of the front of the coat, it had horizontal pocket flaps on the coattails with three buttons, the tails being of a little greater length, namely such that their lower ends were only a hand's breadth higher than the knees, and there was narrow gold galloon around the edges of the shoulder straps. Instead of the previous neckcloths which were black in some regiments and white in others, it was ordered to wear black silk kerchiefs [*platki*], tied in the back. *Gloves* were ordered to be without cuffs. *Canes* remained as before, while new *hats* were authorized, with black plumes of cock feathers. The bow or cockade was of the same ribbon as under the previous reign, with an embroidered gold buttonhole, and with two small silver tassels in the corners, fastened to the ends of a silver cord or length of lace in which, as in the tassels themselves, was intermixed black and orange silk. The hat was prescribed to be 9 5/8 inches tall in front, 10 1/2 inches in back, and the distance from the crown to the corners - 5 1/4 inches (Illus. 1283 and 1284). The *swordknot, sash* [*sharf*], *gorget* [*znak*], and *spontoon* [*esponton*] remain of the previous patterns, except that the last of these had the monogram of Emperor Alexander I, the next to last did not have the cross of St. John of Jerusalem on the eagle's breast, and the swordknot and sash did not have raspberry-colored silk. The color of the spontoon's shaft corresponded to the color of the halberd's shaft. The *greatcoat* was of grey cloth, with a similar hanging cape and also a standing collar of the pattern and color of the coat's (Illus. 1283).

Adjutants [*adyutanty*], of battalions and of honorary colonels, supposed to be of company-grade officer rank, had their entire uniform as well as armament the same as company-grade officers, except for spontoons, which they were not authorized. In formation, when they had to be mounted, they wore deerskin or chamois pants, using ochre to keep them white, and jack boots [*botforty*] with bell-shaped openings and iron spurs (Illus. 1285).

Field-grade officers [*shtab-ofitsery*] were uniformed and armed like adjutants, but they had gilded gorgets (Illus. 1285).

Generals [*generaly*] were distinguished from field-grade officers only by the white plumage around the sides of the hat (Illus. 1286).

Shabracks [*chepraki*] and *holsters* [*chushki*] were the same as before for adjutants, field-grade officers, and generals, of dark-green cloth with one row of gold galloon all around.

Company: barbers [*tsiryulniki*], hospital orderlies [*lazaretnye sluzhiteli*], gunstock craftsman [*lozhnik*], and carpenter [*plotnik*]; battalion clerks [*pisarya*], medics [*fel'dshera*], gunsmith apprentices [*oruzheinye ucheniki*], blacksmiths [*kuznetsy*], and provosts [*profosy*]; regimental wagonmaster [*vagenmeister*], supervisor of the sick [*nadziratel dlya bolnykh*], clerk, chaplains' assistants [*tserkovniki*], gunstock craftsman, and farrier [*konoval*]; and company, battalion, and regimental train personnel [*furleity*], i.e. all *noncombatant* [*nestroevye*] *lower ranks of Grenadier regiments*, wore cloth frock coats [*sertuki*] reaching to the knees, with turned-back skirts, a collar and shoulder straps of the same pattern and color as on the coats of combatant personnel, red kersey lining, and flat brass buttons which were prescribed to be: in front on the right turnover, down the very center of the chest - 6, for the shoulder straps - 1 each, on the cuffs and flaps - 3 each, at the ends of the skirts - 1 each, at the waist - 2; 18 total. The spacing of the buttons down the front was the same as on greatcoats, while the cut and dimensions of the collar, cuffs, flaps, and shoulder straps were as for the coats of combatant lower ranks (Illus. 1287). *Pants* were prescribed to be of grey cloth, but of Flemish linen in summer. *Boots, neckcloth, forage cap, greatcoat, warm coat* or *half-length fur coat, knapsack*, and *water flask* were the same as for combatant lower ranks, while *hats* were of the same pattern and size as described above for officers except without any decoration or trim besides a flat brass button and, serving as binding, a black woolen cord. The wagonmaster, supervisor of the sick, medical orderlies, and all clerks, since they held noncommissioned officer ranks, had gold galloon on the coat's collar and cuffs, gloves with cuffs, cane, and a hanger [*tesak*] with a noncommissioned officer swordknot and a swordbelt (Illus. 1287). Barbers were also authorized swordbelts and hangers, but without swordknots, and on a 1 1/2 inch wide strap over the left shoulder they wore a black leather bag for razors and other items (Illus. 1287). All the rest of the noncombatant lower ranks had no weapons at all (Illus. 1287).

Battalion and *Regimental Doctors* [*lekarya*] received a uniform similar to officers', except that the coat did not have shoulder straps. Collar, cuffs, turnbacks of the coattails, and lining were dark green, with red piping along the edges of the collar, cuffs, flaps on the sleeves and pockets, and turnbacks of the coattails. Silver buttons were located: in front on the right turnover - 6, on the sleeve flaps - 2 each, on the pockets - 3 each, on the ends of the coattails - 1 each, and at the waist - 2. Hat, epee, and swordknot were to be the same as for officers, except without a plume (Illus. 1288).

Auditors [*auditory*] were uniformed similar to doctors, but they had two rows of buttons down the front of the coat; turnbacks of the coattails and lining were red; pants were chamois or deerskin; jackboots with iron spurs; and a hat with the same plume as for officers (Illus. 1288).

6 June 1802— [N.B. See the notes at the end of this volume regarding Grenadiers' distinctive colors - M.C.] Confirmation is given to a list of colors for the **pompons on grenadier caps** (669), based upon which the colors in the directive of 17 March and the table of 30 April, laid out above, which distinguished Grenadier regiments from one another were as follows:

Leib-Grenadier Regiment of the St.-Petersburg Inspectorate:
Red collar and cuffs; red shoulder straps (Illus. 1274); the crowns and bands of grenadier and fusilier caps were red; white pompons with a red center on grenadier caps; pale-yellow [*palevyi*] drumsticks and shafts of halberds and spontoons.

Pavlovsk Grenadier Regiment of the same Inspectorate:
Red collar and cuffs; white shoulder straps; the crowns of grenadier and fusilier caps were red and the bands white; white pompons on grenadier caps (Illus. 1275); pale-yellow drumsticks and shafts of halberds and spontoons.

St.-Petersburg Grenadier Regiment of the Livonia [Livland, Liflyandskaya] Inspectorate:
Turquoise collar and cuffs; red shoulder straps; the crowns of grenadier and fusilier caps were turquoise and the bands red; pompons on grenadier caps were white with a red center (Illus. 1276); pale-yellow drumsticks and shafts of halberds and spontoons.

Taurica Grenadier Regiment of the same Inspectorate:
Turquoise collar and cuffs; white shoulder straps; the crowns of grenadier and fusilier caps were turquoise and the bands white; white pompons on grenadier caps (Illus. 1277); pale-yellow drumsticks and shafts of halberds and spontoons.

Yekaterinoslav Grenadier Regiment of the Lithuania Inspectorate:
Light-green collar and cuffs; red shoulder straps; the crowns of grenadier and fusilier caps were light green and the bands red (Illus. 1278); pompons on grenadier caps were white with a red center; pale-yellow drumsticks and shafts of halberds and spontoons.

Little Russia (Malorossiiskii) Grenadier Regiment of the Ukraine Inspectorate:
Rose collar and cuffs; red shoulder straps; the crowns of grenadier and fusilier caps were rose and the bands red; white pompons on grenadier caps; black drumsticks and shafts of halberds and spontoons (Illus. 1279).

Kiev Grenadier Regiment of the same Inspectorate:
Rose collar and cuffs; white shoulder straps; the crowns of grenadier and fusilier caps were rose and the bands

white; pompons on grenadier caps were white; white drumsticks and shafts of halberds and spontoons (Illus. 1280).

Kherson Grenadier Regiment of the Dniester Inspectorate:

Lilac collar and cuffs; red shoulder straps; the crowns of grenadier and fusilier caps were lilac and the bands red (Illus. 1281 and 1282); pompons on grenadier caps were white with a red center; black drumsticks and shafts of halberds and spontoons.

Siberia Grenadier Regiment of the same Inspectorate:

Lilac collar and cuffs; white shoulder straps; the crowns of grenadier and fusilier caps were lilac and the bands white; pompons on grenadier caps were white; white drumsticks and shafts of halberds and spontoons (Illus. 1280).

Caucasus Grenadier Regiment of the Caucasus Inspectorate:

Blue collar and cuffs; red shoulder straps (Illus 1285); the crowns of grenadier and fusilier caps were blue and the bands red; pompons on grenadier caps were white with a red center; white drumsticks and shafts of halberds and spontoons.

Moscow Grenadier Regiment of the Smolensk Inspectorate:

White collar and cuffs; red shoulder straps (Illus. 1286); the crowns of grenadier and fusilier caps were white and the bands red; pompons on grenadier caps were white with a red center; pale-yellow drumsticks and shafts of halberds and spontoons.

Phanagoria Grenadier Regiment of the Smolensk Inspectorate:

White collar and cuffs; red shoulder straps (Illus. 1287); the crowns of grenadier and fusilier caps were white and the bands red; pompons on grenadier caps were white; white drumsticks and shafts of halberds and spontoons.

Astrakhan Grenadier Regiment of the Moscow Inspectorate:

Orange collar and cuffs; red shoulder straps (Illus. 1287); the crowns of grenadier and fusilier caps were orange and the bands red; pompons on the grenadier caps were white with a red center; white drumsticks and shafts of halberds and spontoons.

18 September 1802 — Lower ranks' **aiguilettes in the Leib-Grenadier Regiment** are abolished, and to replace them they are ordered to have white lace buttonholes on the collar and cuffs (Illus. 1289) (670).

27 October 1802— While on the march with troops or on detached duties, generals and field and company-grade officers are ordered to wear, instead of white pants, **overalls** [*shirovary* (sic, more commonly *sharovary* - M.C.)] or **riding trousers** [*reituzy*]; of grey cloth with flat brass buttons on the side seams, and with black leather lining along down the inner seams and around the lower ends (Illus. 1290) (671).

29 June 1803— New patterns for the ***shabrack*** and ***holster*** are designated for generals, field-grade officers, and adjutants of Grenadier regiments, dark-green as before but with red piping all around, two rows of gold galloon instead of the previous one, and red cloth between these galloon rows (Illus. 1291-2) (672).

19 August 1803— Noncombatant lower ranks of Grenadier regiments are given round **shakos** [*shapki*] in place of the tricorn hat. These are 7 7/8 inches high, of black cloth, with two flaps of similar material sewn inside and used to protect the ears and cheeks during freezing weather. They have a lacquered visor of black leather fastened in three places by small iron hooks and eyes, and a similar black leather chin strap. A black cockade with a surrounding orange stripe and a brass button in the middle is sewn on the front of the shako, and above the cockade are two woolen pompons [*kisti*] of the same colors as were prescribed on 6 June 1802. Between the lower pompon and the cockade button is fastened a loop of black woolen tape (Illus. 1293-4). These shakos are lined upright with straw, quilted through the whole height, while the lower [sic, should be upper? — M.C.] edge is trimmed with black leather. Those holding noncommissioned officer ranks have gold galloon around the upper edge, 7/8 inch wide, and the lower pompon is divided crosswise into four parts, two of which are white and two black with orange, as on grenadier caps for noncommissioned officers (673).

19 October 1803— All noncommissioned officers of Grenadier regiments are to have **two shoulder straps** on their coats and greatcoats as for privates, instead of one (674).

15 November 1804— The Kherson and Siberia Grenadier regiments of the ***Dniester Inspectorate*** are ordered to have: dark-green collars and sleeve flaps with red piping; red cuffs; dark-green crowns to the caps, while the band and shoulder straps remain the same colors as before: in the first regiment - red, in the second - white (Illus. 1295-6) (675). In the same year of 1804, there were introduced for generals and field and company-grade officers of Grenadier regiments ***hats*** [*shlyapy*] with a buttonhole loop of narrow gold galloon, of the pattern used by them on shoulder straps, and with a tall plume (Illus. 1297-8) (676).

26 January 1805— Of the noncommissioned officer strength of second and third battalions of Grenadier regiments, who by the table of 30 April 1802 were supposed to have halberds, four men of each company are ordered to have **muskets and cartridge pouches**, following the example of the situation in the companies of honorary colonels' battalions [*shefskie bataliony*] (677).

13 February 1805— In all Grenadier regiments, the former **grenadier and fusilier caps** of combatant lower ranks are replaced by new ones based on the pattern established in 1803 for noncombatants, except not quilted. There is a brass grenade above the cockade; with a brass button on the chin strap and with a thick horsehair plume. 19 1/4 inches high and about 8 inches wide (Illus. 1299). For privates this plume is completely black and the shako is without any other decoration besides the grenade, cockade, and small pompon (Illus. 1299). For noncommissioned officers the plumes have a white top with a yellow stripe in its middle and the shakos have gold galloon around the top edge of the crown (Illus. 1300-1); for company drummers and for fifers the plumes are red and the shakos are as for privates (Illus. 1302); for battalion and regimental drummers and for musicians the plumes are red with the tops and the shakos as for noncommissioned officers (Illus. 1302) (678).

12 June 1805— For Fusilier battalions of Grenadier regiments, the previously described **shakos** are ordered not to have grenades (679).

23 December 1805— To obviate the inconveniences often met with when in battle with the enemy, generals and field and company-grade officers of regiments of the **Caucasus Inspectorate**, including the Caucasus Grenadier Regiment, are permitted, instead of hats, to wear *shakos*, similar throughout to those of the soldiers except with a silver pompon with a mix of black and orange silk instead of a woolen one. These shakos are to be only for campaigns and military operations, and during other times the above-mentioned ranks are to wear hats (680).

1 July 1806— The flaps over the cuffs are abolished on the coats of **regimental and battalion doctors**, and the cuffs themselves are ordered to be slit instead of round, with two buttons on each, and which as everywhere on the coat are prescribed to be white and flat. Likewise the short boots are replaced by jackboots with spurs. Those holding the rank of staff-doctor [*shtab-lekar*] are given silver embroidered buttonholes, two on each side of the collar and on each cuff (Illus. 1303). Together with this, while on campaign and during operations doctors are permitted to wear grey pants and grey frock coats that are a little below the knees, with dark-green collars and white metal buttons, and sewn so that one coattail goes behind the other. Greatcoats are authorized, likewise grey, with a collar of the same color, having green piping around its edges (Illus. 1304) (681).

1 October 1806— The **warm coats** [*fufaiki*] of lower ranks are discontinued (682).

2 December 1806— Lower ranks are ordered to cut their **hair** short; generals, though, and field and company-grade officers, are in this case allowed to proceed according to their personal wishes (683).

10 March 1807 — Officers' **spontoons and canes** are abolished, and it is ordered that they use **swords** [*shpagi*] while in formation (684).

17 September 1807 — Generals and field and company-grade officers of Grenadier regiments, instead of shoulder straps, are ordered to wear **epaulettes** [*epolety*] with a cloth field the same color as these shoulder straps. One half of the the field, that closest to the collar, is trimmed with narrow gold galloon, and around the edges of the other half are laid two gold cords (Illus. 1305 and 1306). For field-grade officers the epaulettes have a narrow, and for generals a thick, fringe of gold threads (Illus. 1307), and for everyone the epaulettes are passed through a *small shoulder strap* [*pogonchik*] or counter-epaulette [*kontr-epolet*] of the same galloon as on the epaulettes, and are fastened by a button sewn to the coat at the collar (685). Only in the Leib-Grenadier Regiment is it ordered to wear the epaulette only on the left shoulder, as the officers of this regiment have aiguilettes on the right (686).

7 November 1807— For all Army regiments of heavy infantry, **collars and cuffs** of coats, as well as collars of greatcoats, are directed to be of red cloth, while **shoulder straps** are according to the regiment: in the first regiments of each division - red, in the second - white, in the third - yellow, in the fourth - dark green with red piping, and in the fifth - sky blue. In consequence of this, of the Grenadier regiments the Siberia receives white shoulder straps, the St.-Petersburg - yellow, and all the rest - red (687).

15 December 1807— Lower ranks of Grenadier regiments are to have on their **shoulder straps**, and generals and officers on their epaulettes, the number of their division: in gold for the latter and of wool cord for the former: on white and yellow fields - in red, on others - in yellow (688).

19 December 1807 — Lower ranks with **swordbelts** are ordered to wear these not at the waist, but over the right shoulder, under the crossbelt for the pouch, crossing these crossbelts and being of the same width. In consequence of this the former seventh button at the bottom of the coat's front is abolished. Along with this, the swordbelt as well as the crossbelt are to be stitched along their edges and constructed with a small bend so that the upper edges of both one and the other come closer to the collar. The former **swords** [*shpagi*] which have been in use since the time of Empress Anna Ioannovna, with broad blades [*tesachnye klinki*], are replaced by *swords* [*tesaki*] having a hilt with a large, cupped guard, almost the same as for officers' swords [*shpagi*]. With the new swordbelts, bayonet scabbards are fitted into an opening left in the frog to the right of the sword and are parallel to it (Illus. 1308). Beginning at this time, to make them more sturdy, the **shakos** introduced in 1805 were trimmed at the top and on the sides with black leather, and the visor was sewn on, and subsequently they received the name *kiver*(689).

23 December 1807— Lower ranks of Grenadier regiments are ordered to have **winter pants** with leather trim [*obshivka*] on the lower part, in almost the same style as there used to be from 1786 to 1796 (Illus. 1308), while **summer pants** are of Flemish linen, with spats [*kozyrki*] and covered buttons (Illus. 1309). Following this change, the **boots** introduced in 1802 were exchanged for others with soft tops (690).

26 January 1808— Generals of Grenadier regiments at parades, on designated calendar days [*tabelnye dni*], and at troop formations in general, in peacetime as well as during wartime, are ordered to wear the newly introduced **standard generals' coat** [*obshchii generalskii mundir*]. And with the regimental coat when not on duty, they have dark-green pants instead of white (691).

(Note: The description of the standard generals' coat is found later, at the end of the survey of Emperor Alexander I's reign, in the section about general officers' uniforms.)

14 July 1808 — The round **knapsacks** used by lower ranks since 1802 are exchanged for rectangular ones similar to those used during the reign of Emperor Paul I, but of black leather and not made with woolen interiors. They were prescribed to be worn on two soft, whitened deerskin straps, 2 5/8 inches wide, stitched on firmly at the top edge of the back side [of the knapsack - M.C.] and fastened to two large wooden buttons at the bottom edge. A *canteen* [*manerka*] or water flask was strapped to the top of the knapsack, in the middle, with white straps, as previously (Illus. 1310). The knapsack was supposed to contain: 2 shirts, 1 pair of pants, 1 foot wrap, 1 forage cap, material for 1 pair of boots, 1 frizzen cover, 12 flints, 3 brushes, 2 scrapers, 1 small board for cleaning buttons, a small quantity of chalk and polish, a small valise with threads, soap, glue, needlecase with needles, moustache dye, dye comb, sand and a brick, and rusks for three days, so that the valise with the canteen and summer trousers weighed 25 pounds, but with the winter pants (instead of the summer) - 26 1/4 pounds. At the same time it was set forth as a rule that when wearing the knapsack in warm or good weather, the soldier was to have his greatcoat rolled over his left shoulder, with the ends low on his right side being tied with a whitened deerskin strap (Illus. 1310). In cold or inclement weather it was ordered to wear the greatcoat with all its buttons fastened and to take off the coat and place it behind the back above the waist, between the shirt and greatcoat. But in frosts, the coat was to be worn in addition to the greatcoat (622).

Along with this change, the grenadier shakos' former ribbons or cockades were replaced: in Grenadier companies - by a **brass grenade** with three flames, but in Fusilier companies - with one flame. The same grenades were ordered to be on the **pouches**, which from this time began to be made of black, polished leather and smaller than the previous dimensions, the cover being set down as 10 inches long (top) and 7 1/2 inches wide (in the middle) (Illus. 1310) (693).

2 November 1808— The **pants** authorized on 23 December 1807, with leggings [*kragi*] in the winter and spats in the summer, are kept only for combatant lower ranks, while for noncombatants the pants, as well as the boots, are directed to be of the pattern introduced in 1802 (694).

5 November 1808— Company-grade officers of Grenadier regiments, when the troops are wearing **knapsacks**, are ordered to also have them, of the same pattern in all details as was established for lower ranks (695).

12 November 1808— When not on duty, field and company-grade officers are allowed to wear dark-green cloth **pants** instead of white ones (696).

In November 1808— *Officers' gorgets* of a new pattern are confirmed, twice as short as the previous ones, with a raised rim all around and an affixed two-headed eagle in the center. These, as before, are worn on a black ribbon with orange borders, right up against the collar. These gorgets were prescribed for each rank: for an Ensign [*Praporshchik*] - all silver; for a Sublieutenant [*Podporuchik*] - silver with a gold rim; for a Lieutenant [*Poruchik*]- silver with a gold eagle; for a Staff-Captain [*Shtabs-Kapitan*] - silver with a gold rim and a gold eagle; for a Captain [*Kapitan*] - gold with a silver eagle; for field-grade officers - all gold (Illus. 1311) (697).

5 December 1808— **Halberd shafts**, and likewise **drumsticks**, are designated to be yellow in the first regiment of each division, black in the second, white in the third, yellow again in the fourth, and black in the fifth (698).

11 February 1809— Noncombatant lower ranks not holding noncommissioned officer ranks, such as: chaplains' assistants, barbers, hospital orderlies, master craftsmen of every kind, train personnel, and provosts, are all given a new pattern **cap** [*shapka*] in place of the shako [*kiver*], of dark-green cloth, with a red band, also of cloth, a leather chinstrap, two dark-green cloth flaps to cover the ears in winter, and one leather flap to protect the back of the head in inclement weather (Illus. 1312 and 1313) (699).

27 March 1809— Instead of one **epaulette**, officers of the Leib-Grenadier Regiment are ordered to wear two each; **aiguilettes**, however, which have been in use since the reign of Empress Catherine II, are abolished (700).

4 April 1809— **Noncommissioned officers** are ordered to have **galloon** not on the lower and side edges of the collar, but on the upper and side edges .(701)

8 April 1809— There was issued the following order regarding the **shoulder slings on muskets**:

1.) The lower bracket on the stock, for the sling, is to be moved higher up to the brass trigger guard.

2.) The button on the sling is to be located two fingers from the upper sling bracket.

3.) A buckle with prong is to be fixed to the middle of the ramrod's brass lower band or tube.

4.) The upper side, i.e. the side colored red, of the sling is to be lacquered so that it does not stain the pouch crossbelt (702).

20 April 1809— To supplement the directive issued in 1808 concerning new **knapsacks**, the following changes and additions are made:

1.) The **greatcoat** is to be rolled 6 1/2 inches wide and worn over the left shoulder so that the soldier can freely hold the musket behind it.

2.) The lower ends of the greatcoat are to be tied with a strap and buckle 3 1/2 inches from the end.

3.) Greatcoat, knapsack, and canteen straps are not to be whitened.

4.) The left knapsack strap is to be worn over the left shoulder on top of the greatcoat.

5.) To hold both knapsack side-straps, there is another, third, strap with one end sewn to the left side-strap and the other passed through an iron buckle, with a narrow leather loop. The buckle is sewn to the right strap which is bent back under the buckle.

6.) The third, chest, strap is positioned between the first and second top buttons of the coat or greatcoat (Illus. 1314) (703).

30 May 1809 — Noncommissioned officers' front **pouches** [*podsumki*] are replaced with pouches [*sumy*] of the same pattern as prescribed for privates (704).

11 June 1809— **Cords** [*etishkety*] are added to the **shakos** for lower ranks: all white for privates, but for noncommissioned officers and musicians - white with a mixture of black and orange (Illus. 1315) (705).

8 June 1809[sic] — The plumage around the sides of **generals' hats** is discontinued and the former pattern of buttonhole is replaced with a new one made of four thick, twisted cords, of which the two middle ones are intertwined with each other as if in a plait (Illus. 1316) (706).

29 August 1809— Only sergeants [*feldfebeli*] retain the **halberd**, while all other noncommissioned officers are given muskets identical to soldiers'(707).

23 November 1809— Colors are assigned for shako **pompons** [*repeiki*] or tufts of combatant lower ranks: in the 1st battalion - white around, green center; in the 2nd - green around, white center; in the 3rd - red around, yellow center; the colors for noncommissioned officers' pompons are left as before (708).

6 December 1809— Company-grade officers of Grenadier regiments are ordered to wear a ***shako*** [*kiver*] instead of the hat when in formation, of the same pattern and size as those established for lower ranks, but with silver cords with a mixture of black and orange silk, only the tassel and ring being wholly silver. The pompon is silver with an embroidered, silver Imperial monogram in the center surrounded by black and orange small, toothed strips. Flat gilt scales are on the chinstraps, and there is also a small, gilt, six-pointed star behind, which has a small hook attached that during the march or while on campaign is used to take up the long cords and tassels that hang down on the right side of the shako (Illus. 1317). Field-grade officers are given the exact same shakos, but with three rows of thick, silver spangles on the pompon, sewn on around the monogram. These shakos are prescribed to have the exact same three-flamed grenades and the same black hair plumes as privates had, except that the first are gilt. Shakos are not prescribed for generals (709).

In this same year the **powdering of the hair** was completely discontinued for officers, and for them as well as general officers it was permitted to wear, over the coat [*mundir*], double-breasted **frock coats** [*sertuki*] of dark-green cloth, with red cloth collars, red stamin lining, and gilt buttons (Illus. 1318) (710).

9 January 1810— Grenadier regiments are ordered to have **shoulder straps** as follows:

1st Division, Leib-Grenadiers - red. 2nd Div. St.-Petersburg - red. 3rd Div. Taurica - red. 7th Div.Yekaterinoslav - red. 8th Div. Moscow - red. 9th Div. Astrakhan - red. 10th Div. Kiev - red. 11th Div. Siberia - red. 12th Div. Phanagoria - red. 20th Div. Kherson - red. Division Caucasus - white(711).

[Pavlovsk (2nd Div.) and Little Russia (11th Div.) are omitted by Viskovatov. — M.C.]

24 September 1810— **Knapsack straps** are ordered to be stitched on the edges, in the manner of crossbelts and swordbelts, and have a bend at each shoulder so that they do not wear away the coat or constrict a man under his arms (712).

17 January 1811— Instead of the multicolored **cords** on their **shakos**, noncommissioned officers and musicians of Grenadier regiments are to have white ones with only their tassels having black and orange mixed in (Illus. 1319); officers', though, are completely silver (713).

29 January 1811— Officers' **frock coats** are to have red cuffs instead of dark green (714).

3 February 1811 — **Shoulder straps** are ordered to be the same color in all Grenadier regiments - red, with the cursive initial letter of the regiment's name in yellow cord except for the Leib-Grenadier, St.-Petersburg, Graf Arakcheev's, and Little Russia regiments, of which the first is assigned the two Cyrillic letters L.G. the second - S.P., the third – G.A. and the fourth – M.R .(715).

4 February 1811— Grenadiers, Marksmen [*strelki*], and Fusiliers, and in general all combatant ranks including officers, have the shakos' former thick **plumes** replaced with new ones 16 1/2 inches high, 5 3/4 inches wide at the top, and 1 3/4 inches wide at the bottom (Illus. 1319) (716).

22 February 1811— Consequent to the organizational changes of Grenadier regiments, the colors of the **pompons** and **swordknots** are also changed, as follows:

a.) Pompons.

1st battalion, in the 1st Grenadier company - red for Grenadiers, yellow for Marksmen; in the 1st, 2nd and 3rd Fusilier companies - white with a green center (Illus. 1320).

2nd battalion, in the 2nd Grenadier company - red with green below for Grenadiers, yellow with green below for Marksmen; in the 4th, 5th and 6th Fusilier companies - green with a white center (Illus. 1320).

3rd battalion, in the 3rd Grenadier company - red with sky blue below for Grenadiers, yellow with sky blue below for Marksmen; in the 7th, 8th and 9th Fusilier companies - sky blue with a white center (Illus. 1320).

b.) Swordknots.

1st battalion, in the 1st Grenadier company - for Grenadiers, red acorns [*derevyashki*], loops [*gaiki*], and bands [*okolyshi*] or trinchiki, yellow for Marksmen; in the Fusilier comapnies - white acorns with the loops and bands according to the company: in the 1st company - white, in the 2nd - sky blue, and in the 3rd - orange (Illus. 1320).

2nd battalion, in the 2nd Grenadier company - for Grenadiers, red acorns and green loops and bands; for Marksmen, yellow acorns and green loops and bands; in the Fusilier companies - green acorns with the loops and bands according to the company: in the 4th company - white, in the 5th - sky blue, and in the 6th - orange (Illus. 1320).

3rd battalion, in the 3rd Grenadier company - for Grenadiers, red acorns and sky blue loops and bands; for Marskmen, yellow acorns and sky blue loops and bands; in the Fusilier companies - sky blue acorns with the loops and bands according to the company: in the 7th company - white, in the 8th - sky blue, and in the 9th - orange (Illus. 1320). The lace and fringe of swordknots are left white, as before, with black and orange bands for noncommissioned officers (717).

23 September 1811— Combatant lower ranks are ordered to have **forage caps** shaped like shakos, but almost twice as low and without visors, with a red band and the following distinctions:

1st battalion, in the 1st Grenadier company: for Grenadiers - red piping on top; for Marksmen - yellow piping on top and around the band (Illus. 1321).

2nd battalion, in the 2nd Grenadier company: for Grenadiers - green piping on top; for Marksmen - green piping on top and yellow around the band (Illus. 1321).

3rd battalion, in the 3rd Grenadier company: for Grenadiers - sky-blue piping on top; for Marksmen - sky-blue piping on top and yellow around the band (Illus. 1321).

1st battalion, in the 1st, 2nd, and 3rd Fusilier companies - white piping on top and around the band, with the respective number of each company on the front of the band (Illus. 1321).

2nd battalion, in the 4th, 5th, and 6th Fusilier companies - green piping on top and around the band, with the respective number of each company on the front of the band (Illus. 1321).

3rd battalion, in the 7th, 8th, and 9th Fusilier comapnies - sky-blue piping on top and around the band, with the respective number of each company on the front of the band (Illus. 1321) (719).

Officers are given the same caps except with the addition of a sewn-on visor of black, lacquered leather (719). Note by M.C. - the actual decree went as follows:

PSZ No. 24,789. *Forage caps for lower ranks are to be like a shako without a visor, with red bands in Grenadier and infantry regiments and with green bands in Jäger and Marine regiments, in accordance with the models provided to regiments along with their cutters. Different piping on the forage caps, in Grenadier and infantry as well as in Jager and Marine regiments, is to be as follows: Grenadier companies: 1st Grenadier Company, in the grenadier platoon - red piping on the top of the cap, and in the marksmen platoon - yellow piping on the top of the cap and around the band; 2nd Grenadier Company, in the grenadier platoon - green piping on the top of the cap, and in the marksmen platoon - likewise green piping on the top of the cap but yellow around the band; 3rd Grenadier Company, in the grenadier platoon - sky-blue piping on the top of the cap, and in the marksmen platoon - likewise sky-blue piping on the top of the cap but yellow around the band; in the other companies the piping differs by battalion: in the 1st Battalion white piping on the top of the cap and around the band; in the 2nd Battalion green piping on the top of the cap and around the band; in the 3rd Battalion sky-blue piping on the top of the cap and around the band. All these companies, that is to say except for the Grenadier companies, have their company number on the front of the cap band. In Jäger regiments the Grenadier platoons in Grenadier companies are to have red piping around the green band.*

9 October 1811— **Halberds** are withdrawn from all Grenadier regiments, and those sergeants and noncommissioned officers who had them are given soldiers' muskets with bayonets and, consequently, cartridge pouches with crossbelts (720).

3 November 1811— **Gloves** are abolished for noncommissioned officers, and to replace them in winter they are allowed to wear mittens of the same pattern as used at this time by privates (721).

17 December 1811— Noncombatant lower ranks, in place of the frock coats they had since 1802, are given singlebreasted, grey-cloth **caftans** [*kaftany*] or **coats** [*mundiry*] with collar, cuffs, and turnbacks on the tails all that same color, with red piping on them. The existing grey **pants** of these ranks are to also have red piping, in five rows, and leather lining, and are to be worn over the boots. Summer pants are abolished altogether, and grey **forage caps** are to be issued, with earflaps and red piping. Noncombatants holding noncommissioned officer ranks are to keep the gold galloon on their collars and cuffs (Illus. 1322)(722).

1 January 1812— All combatant ranks are given a new pattern *shako* [*kiver*], lower than before, with a greater spread or widening toward the top and indented sides, with flat brass scales on chinstraps; as was already the case for officers, the shako no longer has the sewn-on earflaps and neckflaps (Illus. 1323). Along with this, the previous high, open **collars** are changed to low ones closed in front with small hooks and eyes. The soldiers' integral **leggings** [*kragi*] and the officers' boots are to be high and up to the knees (Illus. 1324), while officers, in order to reduce their expenses, are permitted to have white **shako cords, sashes,** and**swordknots** instead of silver ones, and forged brass appointments on the epaulettes instead of gold (723).

10 February 1812— Noncombatant lower ranks of Grenadier regiments are ordered to have **shoulder straps** on their caftans and greatcoats of the same color and pattern as the shoulder straps of combatant ranks (724).

13 April 1813— The **Kexholm and Pernau Grenadier regiments**, renamed from infantry and assigned to the 1st Division, are authorized grenadier uniform (725).

30 November 1813— For their actions in battle against the enemy, the Yekaterinoslav and Graf Arakcheev Grenadier regiments are granted *badges* [*znaki*] for the shako, of yellow copper or brass, with the raised inscription "For Distinction" [*"Za otlichie"*] (Illus. 1325). This pattern was accepted as standard for all Grenadier regiments which received this award in the subsequent years of Emperor Alexander I's reign (726). (Note: a detailed listing of all regiments which received shako badges with the inscription *"Za otlichie"* will be found later, in a separate paragraph about badges for distinction.)

22 August 1814— **Shoulder straps** in all Grenadier regiments are ordered to be yellow with red letters (727).

In the same year of 1814, during the return of the forces from France, officers of Grenadier regiments were given a new pattern of **riding trousers** [*reituzy*] without leather or buttons, with two wide stripes [*lampasy*] of red cloth along the outer side seams, and on the seam itself — piping of the same material (Illus. 1326). In the following year of 1815, on the **cockades** of officers' hats, along the edges of the black tape with orange teeth, it was ordered to have another white tape of the same width (either of cotton or silk), which in later years became silver (Illus. 1327).

At the same time, ***drum majors*** [*tambur-mazhory*], or the former regimental drummers, were ordered to have shako cords and all lace on the coat in silver or gold, according to the regimental commander's choice, and instead of shoulder straps—epaulettes. These last were authorized to be of the pattern for generals with the only difference being that the galloon around the edges of the cloth field was not entirely silver or gold, but had a red silk stripe down the center. In this uniform, drum majors in formation were authorized a staff [*trost*] with a gilt top in the form of a mace, and with a similar gilt endpiece and silver galloon winding around the staff, ending at the lower end in two silver tassels (Illus. 1328). With the introduction of the new uniform, all musicians, fifers, and drummers, as well as drum majors, were given singlebreasted coats in place of the previous double-breasted ones, these being buttoned in front with small hooks and eyes and having lace not on just one side of the front of the coat, but on both sides (Illus. 1328) (728).

16 August 1815— The **embroidered buttonholes** or bars of lace [*petlitsy*] established in 1802 for officers' coats in those regiments which had Princes of the Blood as Honorary Colonels are to be in only two regiments: His Majesty the Emperor of Austria's Grenadiers and His Majesty the King of Prussia's Grenadiers(729).

7 January 1816— All combatant ranks are forbidden to have the collar of a **shirt** [*rubashka*] or dicky [*manishka*] protruding from behind the neckcloth (730).

24 January 1816— In all Grenadier regiments the **scabbards** for swords [*tesaki*] and bayonets, and consequently those for officers' rapiers [*shpagi*], are ordered to be black, the former being polished and the latter — lacquered (731).

13 April 1816 — Field and company-grade officers of Grenadier regiments are ordered to wear white **pants** (of wool cloth in the winter and linen in the summer) only during reviews and parades, and during the rest of the time to have the riding trousers with stripes prescribed in 1814, with the exception of officers in the capitals, where they are prescribed to be in dark-green pants and high boots (732).

16 April 1817— Instead of grenades, the **shakos** in Grenadier regiments are to have plates of yellow brass with the raised image of an eight-pointed star in the center, with the Imperial Crown on top (Illus. 1329) (733).

7 May 1817— **Drum majors** are ordered to wear coats with silver galloon (734).

13 May 1817— In order to relieve the soldier while on campaign and to protect his accouterments, it is laid down that during this time they are always to be in greatcoats and their shako, plume, pouch, and coat with leggings are to have ***covers*** [*chekhly*] of raven's-duck or Flemish linen painted with black oil paint in the manner of oilcloth so that they do not allow water to penetrate (Illus. 1330 and 1331). Detailed instructions concerning this subject are included in the following:

1.) *For the shako cover.* — The plume, cord, and pompon are removed from the shako; the first is considered below and the rest are stowed in the knapsack. The cover is put on over the shako with visor, it being tailored to fit close, with an overlap on the left side and fastening with small hooks. On the top of the cover where the pompon would be is sewn a piece of cloth the same color as the pompon, and into this pompon cover is inserted a piece of wood. To distinguish companies, company numbers made of yellow cloth are sewn onto the front of the shako covers, designating the first Grenadier company by the letters.1 the second Fusilier company with 1 P.; the second Fusilier company with 2 P., etc. The size of these numbers and letters is 2 1/4 inches. To protect the back of the soldier's head and his ears, an oilcloth, painted on both sides, is to be sewn to the lower edge of the cover in back, its length being determined by the ends of the visor and its width by the height of the shako. In good weather this oilcloth is raised up and its side edges fastened to the cover by small hooks; but in rainy weather it is let down and thus protects the soldier from wetness.

2.) *For the plume cover.* — The plume in its cover is to be worn underneath the sword scabbard with the top pointing down. This cover is to be 21 inches long, i.e. 1 3/4 inches longer than the plume, and its width is according to the plume, with both of its ends having openings tied by drawstrings. The plume in its cover is fastened to the sword by leather loops sewn to the middle and ends of the cover; additionally, the base of the plume is fitted into a hole under the swordbelt frog and tied with a cord to the back of the buckle located on this frog. In order to protect the cover from rubbing on the sword scabbard, both of the cover's ends have a 7/8-inch wide black leather strap lashed to it.

3.) *For the cover for the pouch lid.* — The whole lid of the pouch is to have a cover fitting it closely, going over each edge to the back side for 1 inch, and attached to the pouch by cords: two inside the lid running along it, and two sewn to middle of the upper edge of the cover. On the middle of the lid's cover is to be sewn the company number in yellow cloth.

4.) *For the cover for the coat and leggings.* — The coat must be rolled and wrapped in the leggings [*kragi*] so that it is as long as the knapsack and its diameter is 6 inches in thickness. It is placed into a round oilcloth cover made to these dimensions with an opening at one end that is closed with a drawstring. This case is to be carried on the knapsack with the opening to the left side and in the middle tied by the greatcoat strap to the strap that holds the canteen. And additionally, in the place where the knapsack's shoulder straps pass through, two leather loops are sewn to the cover, through which the greatcoat strap is passed.

All these covers are to be cleaned with a brush and rubbed with a rather strong wax boot polish, so that there is a shine to them; the cloth numbers and letters, on the other hand, are cleaned with ocher (735).

8 August 1817— The size of the **forage cap** is fixed as follows: diameter of the top of the crown - 9 1/2 inches; diameter at the bottom of the crown - according to the size of the head; width of the cap band - 1 1/3 inches; distance from the band to the top of the crown - 2 1/2 inches. Colors are left the same as were laid down on 23 September 1811 (736).

26 September 1817— Confirmed - a description of Grenadier **accouterments** and rules for wearing them, consisting of the following:

1.) *Shako.* - The shako [*kiver*] is to be leather, lined with black cloth for its whole height, while the crown is lacquered. The shako is 7 inches high; the lower diameter is according to the size of the head, while the upper is 4 inches larger. Behind, in the middle, is a black, leather, lacquered strap which dresses the bottom of the shako and is fastened by a rectangular brass buckle stitched to its left end. The width of the leather on the crown, which dresses the top edge of the shako, is 1 1/3 inches, while the width of the four black, lacquered, leather side straps, as well as of the strap which finishes the bottom of the shako, is 7/8 inch. The side straps are stitched to the shako so that the lower, converging, ends are at the very middle of the sides, and between the top ends is a space of 3 1/2 inches. The length of the top edge of the black, leather, lacquered visor - 8 3/4 inches, and the width down its center - 2 1/2 inches. It is sewn to the lower edge of the shako in the center front, under the strap which edges the bottom of the shako (Illus. 1332).

2.) *Shako plate and badge for distinction.* - The plate [*blyakha*] must be of yellow brass, fitted so that its top end is right under the stitching of the leather crown, touching the very middle of the badge for distinction [*znak otlichiya*]. But so that this last item cannot bend or break, it is seated on hard shoe-sole leather fixed to the badge for distinction by prongs attached to badge's inner side for this purpose (Illus. 1332).

3.) *Shako pompon.* - The pompon [*repeek*] is to be of wood, oval, and lined with cloth; colors are according to the battalion and company as laid down in 1811. It is 3 inches long, 1 3/4 inches wide in the middle, and swells to 7/8 inch high in the center. In regiments without a badge for distinction, the lower end of the shako pompon must be even with the stitching of the leather crown; in regiments with them, though, it is over the badge, covering its lower rim (Illus. 1332).

4.) *Shako cords.* - The cords [*etishkety*] are to be made from white cords: for noncommissioned officers - with tassels of orange and black worsted and white silk, and for privates - all white. They hang on the shako in front and in back in half-circles, having the upper ends at the very middle of the shako's sides, 1/2 inch from the top of the crown, while the lower plaits of the half-circles are over the upper stitching of the leather strap which finishes the bottom of the shako. The front plaits are 1 1/3 inches wide and the back ones 7/8 inch. The first tassel of the cord dropping from the right side hangs from four small cords level with the right shoulder, while the tassel on the left side cord hangs from two small cords even with the leather strap which dresses the top of the shako (Illus. 1332).

5.) *Shako scales.* - Scales [*cheshuya*] on the shako are to consist of 18 pieces on each side, seated at equal intervals on a black leather strap that is not backed by any harder material. The upper end of the scales is to be between the shako's side straps, 1 1/3 inches from the stitching of the bottom strap, and is fastened by a brass circlet with prongs pushed through the shako and bent over on the inside. Underneath the chin the scales are fastened together by a wooden toggle (Illus. 1332).

6.) *Shako plume.* - The length of the hair plume [*sultan*], the black one of noncommissioned officers and soldiers as well as the red one of musicians, is to be 19 inches; their diameter: at the bottom - 1 3/4 inches, at the top - 3 1/2 inches, and the length of the white top part of a noncommissioned officer's plume - 5 1/4 inches. The plume up the hair itself is stuck into a hollow fitting on the shako, and the fitting is stitched from black, lacquered leather to the middle of the front of the shako with the top end even with the top of the crown and the lower end under the plate, so that it is covered by it (Illus. 1332).

7.) *Swordbelt and crossbelt.* - Swordbelts and crossbelts [*portupei i pervyazi*] are white deerskin and 3 1/2 inches wide between the edges and 2 1/4 inches wide between the stitchings. In order to keep them in the proper position when a soldier moves about, there is a leather button under the swordbelt at the point on the chest where the belts cross, and under the crossbelt - a buttonhole, through which this button is fastened. In the same manner, on the back of the left side of pouch on the upper edge there is a white leather loop with a cutout shaped like a single-flamed grenade, and on the swordbelt, to fasten to this loop, is fixed a leather button. The swordbelt frog is to be as wide as the sword scabbard. For bayonets, the swords have a small tube under the swordbelt and above the frog, stitched from soft leather, as wide as the bayonet scabbard. The distance of the rectangular brass swordbelt buckle from the frog is to be such that it is as close to the frog as possible and almost not visible. The buckle is to be of yellow brass (Illus. 1333).

8.) *Swords.* - The hilts of the swords [*tesaki*] are to be of yellow brass, while the scabbards, just as the bayonet scabbards, are to be of black, polished leather (Illus. 1333).

9.) *Pouch.* - Pouches [*sumy*] are to be be of black leather with the sides and lid lacquered. Its size is to be enough to freely hold sixty live cartridges laid in a cotton case. To the pouch's box, under the lid, there is to be stitched a small pouch of soft black leather, with a small cover flap fastened by a small leather button. This is for keeping wadding, a screwdriver, priming wire, and a spare flint. The handle of the screwdriver must be made as flat as practicable so that the pouch lid can closely fastened. The lid of this pouch is to be semicircular and fastened to the box by a leather loop over a small leather button, and in its center is fixed a three-flamed grenade of yellow brass (Illus. 1333).

10.) *The wearing of the sword and pouch* - The sword and pouch are to be worn so that if the soldier bends his left elbow then the top end of the sword and the top edge of the pouch would be 3 1/2 inches below this elbow. However, in a frontal formation this rule applies only to the two flank files, i.e. the first and the last, while the rest are aligned with them by a cord (Illus. 1333).

11.) *Swordknots.* - Swordknots [*temlyaki*] are to be of the battalion and company colors defined in 1811, having linen lace with the rest of wool. The lace is 7/8 inch wide; its length is to be such that after it is wrapped around the hilt, there is left a distance of 1 3/4 inches from the hilt to the swordknot's small button (Illus. 1333).

12.) *The rolled greatcoat.* - The greatcoat is to be rolled over its whole width and worn over the left shoulder, its length to be determined by the length of the straightened right arm. But in this case, too, in a frontal formation a cord is used as in § 10. The end of the greatcoat is to be opposite the end of the right thigh; width: on the shoulder - 5 1/4 inches, on the chest - 4 1/2 inches, at the end - 3 1/2 inches; the distance from the lower end to the greatcoat strap - 1 3/4 inches; width of the this last item - 7/8 inch, with its buckle being rectangular and of iron (Illus. 1333 and 1334).

13. *Knapsack.* - Knapsacks [*rantsy*] are to be of calfskin leather with the hair still on, with a linen lining. The length of the knapsack - 16 inches; height - 12 inches; thickness - 4 1/2 inches; length of the cover, from the upper edge - 10 1/2 inches. This last item is to be closed by three rectangular iron buckles 7/8 inch wide. The black leather strap which fastens the middle buckle is to be stitched onto the center of the knapsack cover so it can be attached to the canteen, while the other two straps are stitched onto the edges below this cover. A black leather loop is sewn above the middle buckle, through which is passed the strap for fastening. The knapsack shoulder straps are 7/8 inch wide while the chest strap is 1 1/3 inches; the chest buckle is rectangular and of iron. The knapsack is worn close to the back, having its upper edge level with the shoulders. The top ends of the knapsack shoulder straps must be fastened, with a distance of 1 3/4 inches from one to the other, to two leather loops sewn on the back of the knapsack at the middle of its upper edge, while the lower ends of these straps are fastened to oblong wooden toggles fixed to the lower corners of the knapsack. These straps are to be around the soldier's shoulder in the shape of a half circle: on the left shoulder - over the rolled greatcoat, and on the right - over the shoulder strap. And to the centers of these half circles are sewn: on the left - the chest strap, and to the right - a leather loop with the chest buckle to which the strap is fastened, making sure that it is on the chest and even with the armpits (Illus. 1333 and 1334). Inside the knapsack, running along its whole length, is a linen divider separating it into two halves. In the first of these, on the side facing the canteen, are placed: rusks for three days and one pair of soles, upright; in the second - pants (winter ones during summer and summer ones during winter), wool socks and foot wraps; a small valise with a needlecase, scissors, penknife, thread, thimble, awls, wax-end, soap, polish, brick, comb for the head, dye and an iron dye comb, earmuffs, neckcloth, mittens (in summer); brushes for clothes, underclothes, and boots (upright next to the sides of the knapsack); flint case with 12 flints; two scrapers for cleaning the musket, a small board for cleaning buttons, boot material, two shirts, forage cap, and frizzen cover.

14.) *Canteen.* - The canteen [*manerka*] is of white sheet iron, held to the knapsack by whitened deerskin straps, 7/8 inch wide, so that the lower edge of its lid is even with the top of the knapsack. To begin attaching the canteen, a loop is taken, made from a strap as long as the knapsack is thick, and is fastened behind this last item at the loop to which are tied the knapsack shoulder straps. After this, the canteen strap is passed through this loop and under the middle one of straps on the knapsack cover, and, passing through the canteen ear tabs, is fastened beneath it, again under the middle knapsack cover strap, with an iron, rectangular buckle. The canteen lid is also to be attached to a strap, the top end of which is slit to form a buttonhole and fastened to the lid's ear tab on the right side with a small leather button, while the lower end reaches to the middle of the right side of the canteen and is stitched to a loop which freely moves along the canteen's side strap (Illus. 1333 and 1334).

15.) *Entrenching tool.* - The entrenching tool [*shantsovyi instrument*] is to be carried in a case of black, polished leather, on a whitened deerskin strap 1 1/3 inches wide, on top of the full accouterments, over the left shoulder (Illus. 1333 and 1334).

16.) *Stitching on belts.* - Swordbelts, crossbelts, and all straps and belts in general, such as those for the greatcoat, the shoulder and chest straps of the knapsack, and the canteen and entrenching tool straps, are determined to have stitching [*strochenie*] (Illus. 1333 and 1334).

17.) *Drummers' crossbelt.* - Drummers' crossbelts [*barabannyya perevyazi*] are to be white deerskin and under the right shoulder strap. Width: from one edge to the other - 4 3/8 inches; between stitchings - 3 inches. There is an elongated cutout at the shoulder, 7 inches long and 7/8 inch wide in the middle. 5 1/4 inches below this cutout is set a brass plate with two tubular holders for the drumsticks, its length to be 5 1/4 inches and its width 4 3/8 inches. Three grenades are set on the crossbelt 1/2 inch above the plate, single flamed, made of yellow brass, and placed so that the edges of the two lower ones are at the stitchings and the third is in the center of the crossbelt, 1/2 inch above the ends of the first two (Illus. 1335). So that they may better carry their drums during marches, drummers are to wear the knapsack behind the left shoulder on a strap going over the right one, so that the top edge of the end is 1 3/4 inches above the coat's waistline, in back. This strap, 2 5/8 inches wide and long enough to fit the man's size, is to be worn under the shoulder strap, fastened to the knapsack by two elongated wooden toggles which are to be attached to the sides of the knapsack 4 1/2 inches from its upper edge (737).

The instructions about the shako pattern as set forth above are also extended to officers (Illus. 1336).

8 December 1817— The leather **leggings** [*kragi*] on the cloth pants in Grenadier regiments are ordered to have **integral spats** [*kozyrki*] of a pattern similar to the gaiter spats [*shtibletnye kozyrki*] of summer pants(738).

2 March 1818 — Uniforms, accouterments, and armament of the patterns in use at this time in other Grenadier regiments are given to the 1st and 2nd Grenadier regiments established in the **Separate Lithuania Corps**, except with white appointments instead of yellow, yellow cloth everywhere in place of red, yellow cuff flaps instead of dark green, and the addition of yellow lapels (Illus. 1337 and 1338). Shoulder straps are also yellow, with the number in red. For officers the buttons are flat and on their gorgets, instead of St. George the Bearer of Victory being on the eagle's breast shield, there is an representation of a Lithuanian horseman (739).

20 June 1818— With the Pernau Grenadier Regiment being renamed the **Crown Prince of Prussia's**, sholder straps and epaulettes in this regiment are ordered to have a monogram of the letters: K.P.F.W. (740).

23 August 1818— Combatant lower ranks of Grenadier regiments are to have **shoulder straps** on coats and greatcoats that are as long as the shoulder and 2 1/8 inches wide, of the previous yellow color, with a cursive initial letter of the regiment 1 3/4 inches in size, cut out 7/8 inch from the lower edge of shoulder strap and backed with red cloth stiched around the edges of the cutout. The flaps or **wings** [*klapany ili kryltsa*] over the shoulders of musicians' and drummers' coats are prescribed to be of red cloth, while the tape for sewn-on trim, 7/8 inch wide, is white with a red stripe down the center (Illus. 1339) (741).

25 January 1819— **Drumsticks** and **entrenching tool handles** are directed to be: in the first regiments of a division - pale yellow; in the second regiments - black; in the third - white; and in the fourth - light brown (742).

4 April 1819— The **spats** on the leggings since 1817 are abolished (743).

10 April 1819— The *hornists* [*gornisty*] and *signalers* [*signalisty*] newly placed on the establishment of Grenadier regiments are authorized the same uniform as for drummers, and the *signal horns* [*signalnye rozhki*] are to be of yellow brass, with white straps, and painted inside with red paint, with a gold wreath around the edge (Illus. 1340) (744).

20 September 1820— Field and company-grade officers of Grenadier regiments are given new pattern *gorgets* [*znaki*], flatter and narrower than before, without a ribbon, this being replaced by two loops of gold cord, these being fixed at one end to two small gold buttons and passed through holes in the ends of the gorget, while the other end is held by the buttons on the epaulettes (Illus. 1341) (745).

In this same year of 1820 there were changes in **musicians' and drummers' coats** which consisted of the tape on them beginning to be sewn on almost touching each other, and on the wings it was already not straight to the lower edge, as before, but slanted; it also began to be sewn around all four edges of the collar (Illus. 1342) (746).

26 November 1823— In Grenadier regiments all **musicians**, even though they might not hold noncommissioned officer ranks, were ordered to have: gold galloon on the coat; plumes on the shakos with noncommissioned officers's tops and noncommissioned officers' pompons. This was not applied to hornists, fifers, or drummers who did not hold noncommissioned officer rank (747).

16 January 1824 — The following changes are ordered to be carried out in the uniforms and accouterments of combatant lower ranks:

1.) **Coattails**, which up to this had one covering the other, are to be cut so that their inner edges come together, and sewn together so they touch.

2.) The decorative end [*trinchik*] of the **shako cords**, which is to be level with the right shoulder, is to have another special loop of white cord attached to the button on the right shoulder strap, so that the shako cords stay in place when the soldier moves about.

3.) The **cartridge pouch** is to be worn so that when the soldier bends his elbow, the distance between it and the line of the top edge of the pouch is equal to 5 1/4 inches.

4.) **Knapsack chest straps** are to be fitted so that they are between the fourth and fifth buttons of the coat, as counted from the collar.

5.) On the **musket sling**, opposite the cocking piece, there is to be a band of the same kind of leather as the sling, for stowing the firing cover [*ognivnyi chekhol*] when it needs to be taken off (Illus. 1343) (748).

29 March 1825— For noncombatant [sic – should be "combatant" – M.C.] lower ranks, for faultless service, are established **stripes** [*nashivki*] to be sewn on the left sleeve: for 10 years service - one, for 15 years - two, for 20 years - three; one over the other, all of yellow tape (749).

NOTES

(665) Polnoe Sobranie Zakonov Rossiiskoi Imperii (Complete Collection of Laws of the Russian Empire, hereafter cited as PSZ), vol. XXVI, pg. 609, No19,826.

(666) PSZ, vol. XLIV, pg. 72, No19,950.

(667) PSZ, vol. XLIV, chap II, instructions for coats, pp. 29 and 59, No20,109.

(668) Ibid., pg. 30, No20,186.

(669) Ibid., pg. 64, No20,287.

(670) From transactions in the Archives of the Commissariat Department of the Ministry of War.

(671) Ibid., pg. 30, No20,485.

(672) PSZ, vol. XXVII, pg. 415, No21,377, and evidence from contemporaries.

(673) From transactions in the Archives of the Commissariat Department of the Ministry of War, pg. 67, No20,927, and an actual model headdress preserved at the Commissariat Department of the Ministry of War.

(674) Instruction of the Military College, 20 October 1803.

(675) From transactions in the Archives of the Commissariat Department of the Ministry of War.

(676) Model officer's hat from that time, preserved in the Personal Arsenal of the SOVEREIGN EMPEROR in the Anichkovsk Palace; drawings of 1804-model coats, kept in HIS IMPERIAL MAJESTY'S Personal Library under No361, and evidence from contemporaries.

(677) PSZ, vol. XXVIII, pg. 794, No21,603.

(678) PSZ, vol. XLIV, pg. 67, No21,621; shakos with similar plumes, preserved in the Personal Arsenals of the SOVEREIGN EMPEROR and His Imperial Highness the Grand Duke Michael Pavlovich, and evidence from contemporaries.

(679) Announcement of the Government Military College to the Military Commissariat, 12 June 1805.

(680) PSZ, vol. XLIV, pg. 67, No21,969.

(681) PSZ, vol. XLIV, pg. 31, No22,197.

(682) From transactions in the Archives of the Commissariat Department of the Ministry of War.

(683) PSZ, vol. XXIX, pg. 201, No22,382.

(684) PSZ, vol. XXIX, pg. 1039, No21,482, and evidence from contemporaries.

(685) and (686) PSZ, vol. XLIV, pg. 14, No22,625, and evidence from contemporaries.

(687) PSZ, vol. XLIV, pg. 67, No22,677.

(689) PSZ, vol. XLIV, pg. 13, No22,720; actual articles preserved in various Arsenals, and evidence from contemporaries.

(690) PSZ, vol. XLIV, pg. 67, No22,720.

(691) PSZ, vol. XXX, pg. 45, No22,784.

(692) and (693) Archive of the Inspection Department of the Ministry of War, transactions upon the suggestion of the Honorable Minister of War, with drawings and descriptions: the manner in which to wear knapsacks and greatcoats, 1808, No13786/654, and evidence from contemporaries.

(694) PSZ, vol. XLIV, part II, pg. 67, No23,335.

(695) PSZ, vol. XXX, pg. 669, No23,343.

(696) From transactions in the Archive of the Commisariat Department of the Ministry of War.

(697) PSZ, vol. XLIV, part II,pg. 31, No23,377; actual gorgets preserved in the Personal Arsenal of the SOVEREIGN EMPEROR, and evidence from contemporaries.

(698) PSZ, vol. XLIV, pg. 68, No23,382.

(699) PSZ, vol. XXX, pg. 781, No23,478, and headdress specimens at the Commissariat Department, No119.

(700) PSZ, vol. XLIV, pg. 13, No23,548.

(701) From transactions in the Archive of the Commissariat Department of the Ministry of War.

(702) PSZ, vol. XXX, pg. 904, No23,571.

(703) PSZ, vol. XXX, pg. 950, No23,625.

(704) PSZ, vol. XXX, pg. 970, No23,667.

(705) PSZ, vol. XLIV, pg. 31, No23,736.

(706) PSZ, vol. XXX, pg. 1006, No23,695.

(707) PSZ, vol. XXX, pg. 1114, No23,812.

(708) PSZ, vol. XLIV, pg. 68, No24,000.

(709) and (710) PSZ, vol. XXX, pp. 1364/1362, No24049/24019; Model shako confirmed by Highest Authority, 15 December 1809, located in the Personal Arsenal of HIS IMPERIAL MAJESTY, in the Anichkovsk Palace, and evidence from contemporaries.

(711) PSZ, vol. XLIV, pg. 68, No24,113.

(712) PSZ, vol. XXXI, pg. 362, No24,357.

(713) PSZ, vol. XXXI, pg. 517, No24,488, and evidence from contemporaries.

(714) From transactions in the Archive of the Commissariat Department of the Ministry of War.

(715) From transactions in the Archive of the Commissariat Department of the Ministry of War.

(716) PSZ, vol. XLIV, pg. 69, No24,529, and an actual model plume preserved at the Commissariat Department.

(717) PSZ, vol. XXXI, pg. 558, No24,527.

(718) PSZ, vol. XLIV, pg. 69, No24,789.

(719) Evidence from contemporaries.

(720) PSZ, vol. XXXI, pg. 862, No24,805.

(721) PSZ, vol. XLIV, pg. 898, No24,848.

(722) PSZ, vol. XLIV, pg. 31, No24,911 and 24,912, and evidence from contemporaries.

(723) From transactions in the Archive of the Commissariat Department of the Ministry of War and evidence from contemporaries.

(724) PSZ, vol. XLIV, pg. 70, No24,991.

(725) PSZ, vol. XXXII, pg. 556, No25,370.

(726) Highest Order and actual badges for distinction preserved in various Arsenals and at the Commissariat Department of the Ministry of War.

(727) Highest Order.

(728) Evidence of contemporaries and actual uniforms from that time preserved in various Arsenals and at the Commissariat Department of the Ministry of War.

(729) From transactions in the Archive of the Commissariat Department of the Ministry of War.

(730) PSZ, vol. XXXIII, pg. 430, No26,063.

(731) Highest Order and evidence from contemporaries.

(732) From transactions in the Archive of the Commissariat Department of the Ministry of War.

(733) PSZ, vol. XLIV, pg. 138, No26,801.

(734) PSZ, vol. XLIV, pg. 120, No26,833.

(735) PSZ, vol. XLIV, part II, pp. 112 and 120, No26,857.

(736) PSZ, vol. XLIV, part II, pg. 104, No26,842.

(737) PSZ, vol. XLIV, part II, pg. 104, No27,067.

(738), (739), and (740) From transactions in the Archive of the Commissariat Department of the Ministry of War.

(741) PSZ, vol. XLIV, part II, pg. 121, No27,504.

(742) PSZ, vol. XLIV, part II, pg. 108, No27,653.

(743), (744), (745), and (746) From transactions in the Archive of the Commissariat Department of the Ministry of War.

(747) Order to the Separate Corps of Military Settlements, 26 November 1823, No49.

(748) From transactions in the Archive of the Commissariat Department of the Ministry of War.

(749) Order to the Separate Corps of Military Settlements, 16 January 1824, No22.

РИСУНКИ
ОДЕЖДЫ и ВООРУЖЕНІЯ
РОССІЙСКИХЪ
ВОЙСКЪ
1801-1825.

PLATES LIST OF ILLUSTRATIONS

1321. Forage Caps of Combatant Lower Ranks. From 1811 on.

1322. Noncombatants. 1811-1824.

1323. Grenadiers' Shakos. 1812-1816.

1324. Company-grade Officer and Noncommissioned Officer. Grenadier Regiments. 1812-1816.

1325. Shako Badge for Distinction, confirmed in 1813.

1326. Company-grade Officer. Grenadier Regiments. 1814-1816.

1327. Officers' Hat. From 1815 on.

1328. Drum Major. Grenadier Regiments. 1815-1817.

1329. Grenadiers' Shako Plate. 1817-1828.

1330. Grenadiers. 1817-1824.

1331. Grenadier. 1817-1824.

1332. Grenadiers' and Noncommissioned Officers' Shakos. 1817-1828.

1333. Grenadiers. Grenadier Regiments. 1817-1824.

1334. Grenadier. Grenadier Regiments. 1817-1824.

1335. Drummer. Grenadier Regiments. 1817 and 1818.

1336. Company-grade Officer. H.M. the Emperor of Austria's and H.M. the King of Prussia's Grenadier Regiments. 1817-1826.

1337. Grenadier. Grenadier Regiments of the Separate Lithuania Corps. 1818-1826.

1338. Field-grade Officer. Grenadier Regiments of the Separate Lithuania Corps. 1818-1826.

1339. Fifers. Grenadier Regiments. 1818-1820.

1340. Hornists. Grenadier Regiments. 1819-1820.

1341. Officers' Gorget, confirmed 1820.

1342. Drummer. Grenadier Regiments. 1820-1826.

1343. Noncommissioned Officer. Marksmen Platoons of Grenadier Regiments. 1824-1826.

Emperor Alexander I

Grenadiers. Leib-Grenadier Regiment of the St.-Petersburg Inspectorate. 1802.

Grenadier Cap. Pavlov Grenadier Regiment of the St.-Petersburg Inspectorate. 1802-1813.

Grenadiers. St.-Petersburg Grenadier Regiment of the Liflyand Inspectorate. 1802-1805.

Grenadiers. Taurica Grenadier Regiment of the Liflyand Inspectorate. 1802-1805.

Noncommissioned Officers. Yekaterinoslav Grenadier Regiment of the Lithuanian Inspectorate.
1802-1805.

1279.

Fifer and Drummer of Grenadier Companies. Little Russia Grenadier Regiment of the Ukraine Inspectorate. 1802-1805

53

Battalion Drummers. Kiev Grenadier Regiment of the Ukraine Inspectorate. 1802-1805.

Fusilier Caps. Kherson Grenadier Regiment of the Dniester Inspectorate. 1802-1804.

Fusiliers. Kherson Grenadier Regiment of the Dniester Inspectorate. 1802-1804.

Company-grade Officers. Siberia Grenadier Regiment of the Ukraine Inspectorate. 1802-1804.

Hat for Field and Company-grade Officers. 1802-1804.

Field-grade Officer and Adjutant. Caucasus Grenadier Regiment of the Caucasus Inspectorate. 1802-1804.

General. Moscow Grenadier Regiment of the Smolensk Inspectorate. 1802-1804.

1287.

Clerk, Barber, and Driver. Phanagoria and Astrakhan Grenadier Regiments of the Smolensk and Moscow Inspectorates. 1802-1803.

1288.

Doctor and Auditor. 1802-1804.

Grenadier. Leib-Grenadier Regiment. 1802-1805.

1290.

Officers. Leib-Grenadier Regiment. 1802-1804. (In campaign uniform.)

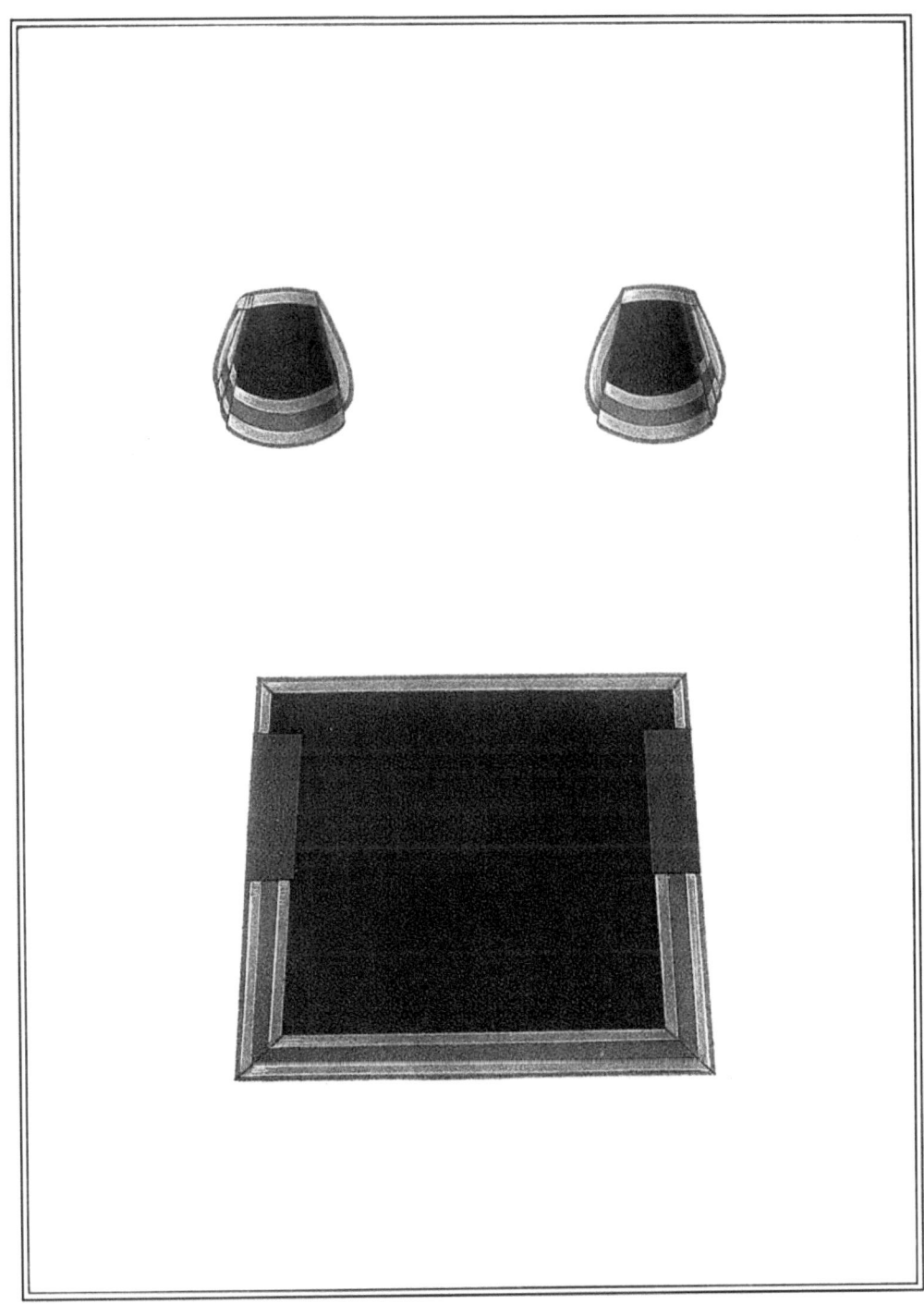

Officers' Shabrack and Holsters for Grenadier Regiments. From 1802 on.

Рис. на кам. Пашенный.

Shako for Noncombatant Lower Ranks. 1803-1809.

Fusilier Noncommissioned Officers. Kherson and Siberia Grenadier Regiments
of the Dniester Inspectorate. 1804-1805.

Officers' Hat. 1804-1816.

Grenadier Shako. 1805-1807.

Noncommissioned Officer. Grenadier Regiments. 1805-1807.

Company Drummer and Musician. Grenadier Regiments. 1805-1807.

1303.

Staff-Doctor and Doctor. 1806-1811.

Составл. Губаревъ и Вишневскій.   Рис. на кам. Петровой.

Doctors. 1806-1811.

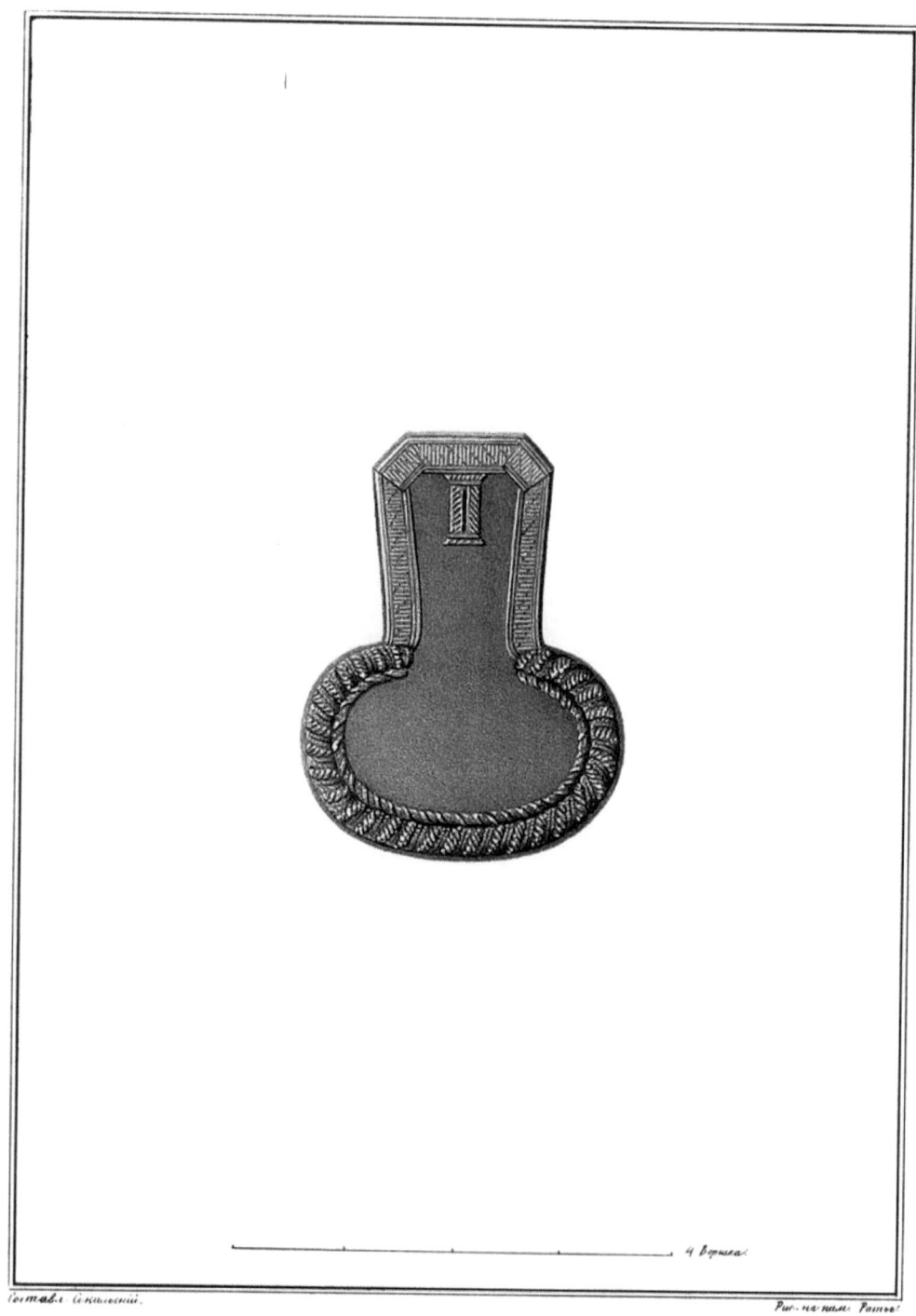

Company-grade Officers' Epaulette, confirmed in 1807.

1306.

Company-grade Officer. Grenadier Regiments. 1807-1811.

Field-grade Officer and General. Grenadier Regiments. 1807-1811.

Grenadiers. 1807-1808.

Grenadiers. 1807-1808.

Grenadiers. 1807-1808.

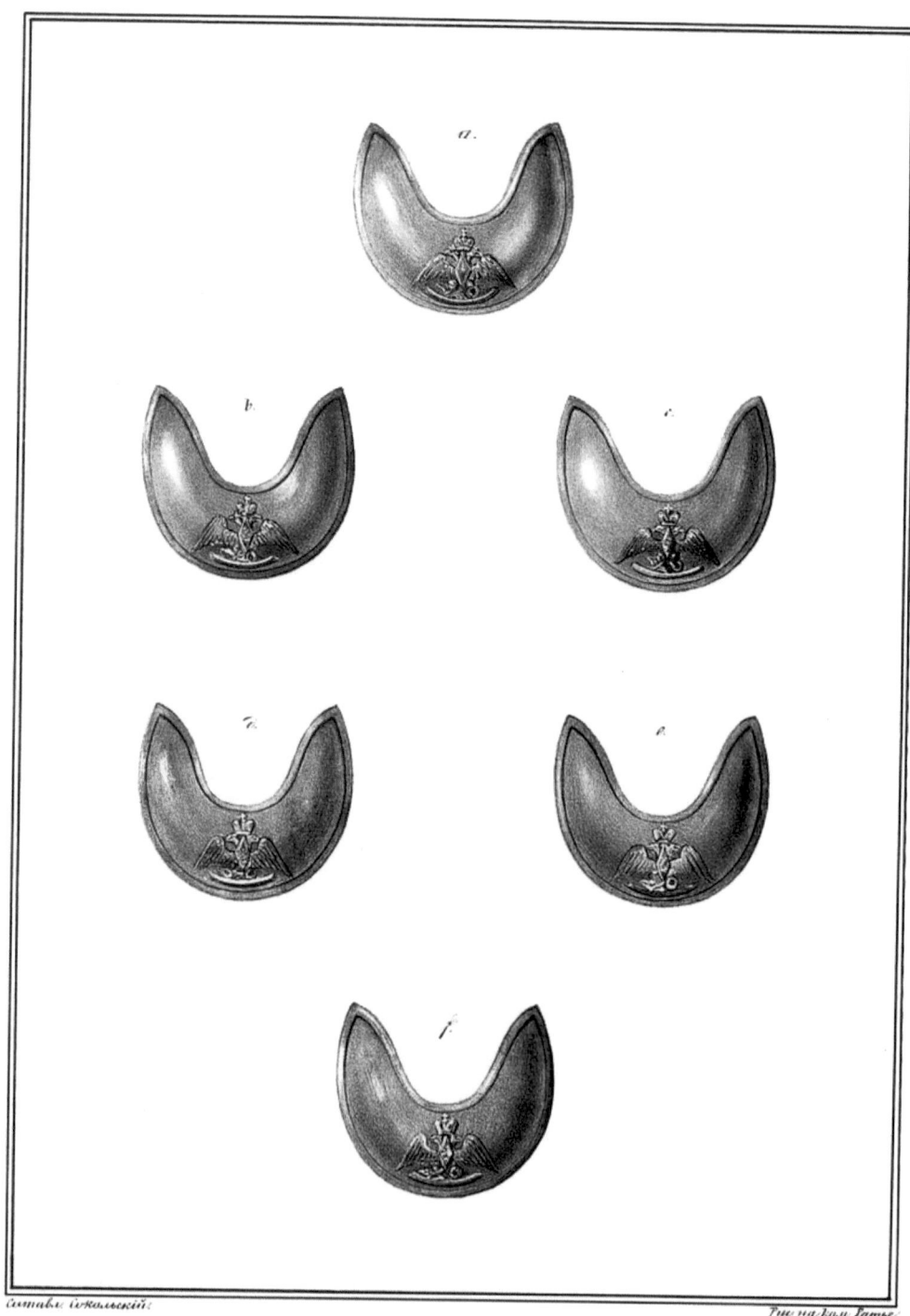

Officers' Gorgets. 1808-1820.

Train Personnel. 1809-1811.

1313.

Состави. Захаровъ   Рис. на кам. Гиллеръ.

Hat for Noncombatant Lower Ranks. 1809-1811.

Grenadier. 1809.

Grenadier Shako for Noncommissioned Officers and Privates. 1809-1811.

Составл. Петровъ.   Рис. на Кам. Пашенный

Generals' Hat. 1809-1815.

Officers' Shako for Grenadier Regiments. 1809-1811.

1318.

Field-grade Officer. Grenadier Regiments. 1809 and 1810.

Составл. Петровъ   Рис на кам. Пашенный.

Noncommissioned Officers' Shako for Grenadier Regiments. 1811.

Infantry Pompons and Swordknots for Lower Ranks. 1811-1833.

1321.

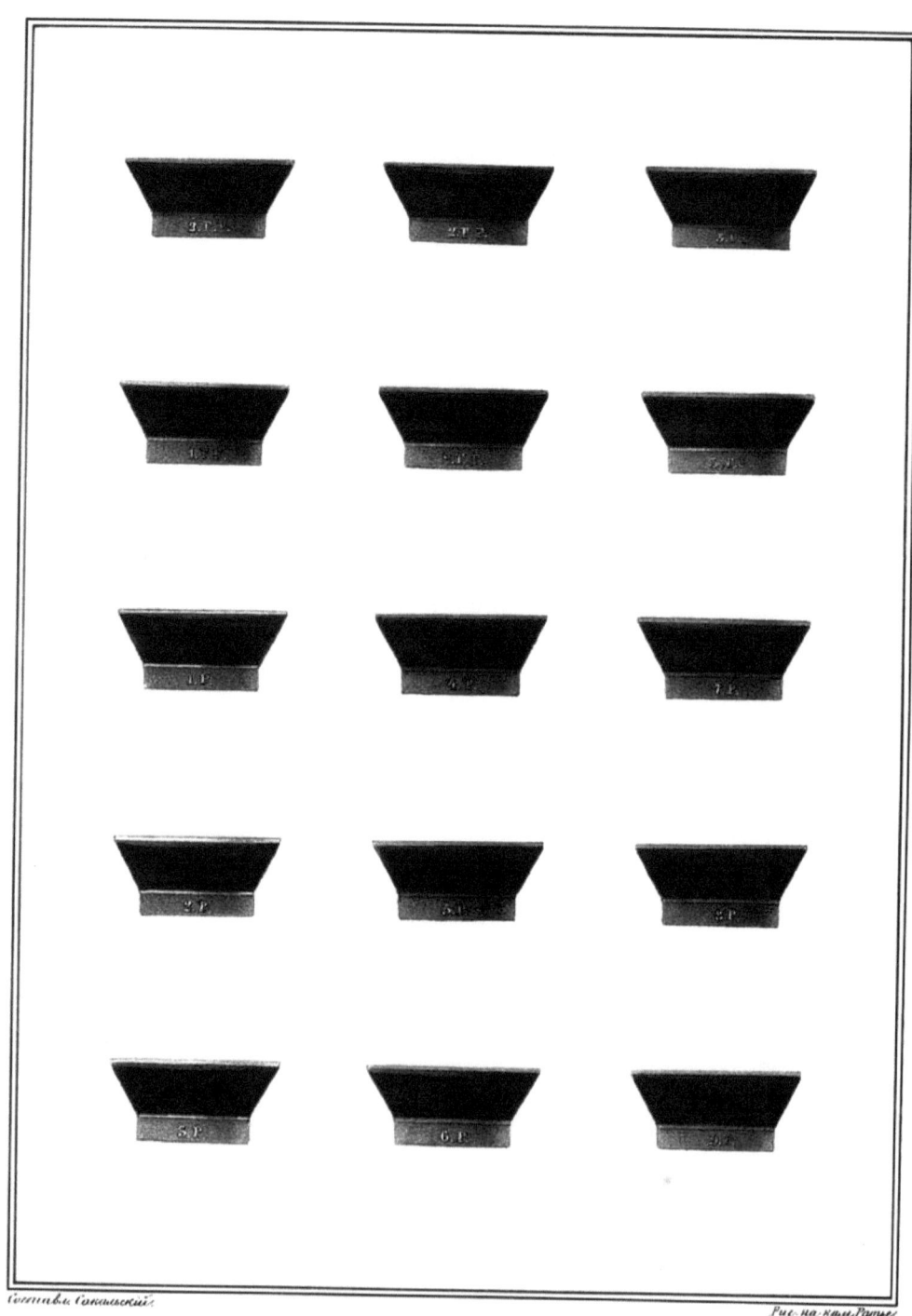

Forage Caps of Combatant Lower Ranks. From 1811 on.

Составл. Губаревъ и Разумихинъ.   Рис. накам. Фернхендъ.

Noncombatants. 1811-1824.

Grenadiers' Shakos. 1812-1816.

1324.

Company-grade Officer and Noncommissioned Officer. Grenadier Regiments. 1812-1816.

ЗА ОТЛИЧІЕ

Shako Badge for Distinction, confirmed in 1813.

Company-grade Officer. Grenadier Regiments. 1814-1816.

Officers' Hat. From 1815 on.

Drum Major. Grenadier Regiments. 1815-1817.

Grenadiers' Shako Plate. 1817-1828.

Grenadiers. 1817-1824.

Grenadiers. 1817-1824.

1332.

Grenadiers' and Noncommissioned Officers' Shakos. 1817-1828.

Grenadiers. Grenadier Regiments. 1817-1824.

Составл. Петровъ

Рис. на кам. Андерсонъ и Бѣлоусовъ.

Grenadiers. Grenadier Regiments. 1817-1824.

Drummer. Grenadier Regiments. 1817 and 1818.

Company-grade Officer. H.M. the Emperor of Austria's and H.M. the King of Prussia's Grenadier Regiments. 1817-1826.

Grenadier. Grenadier Regiments of the Separate Lithuania Corps. 1818-1826.

Field-grade Officer. Grenadier Regiments of the Separate Lithuania Corps. 1818-1826.

1339.

Fifers. Grenadier Regiments. 1818-1820.

Hornists. Grenadier Regiments. 1819-1820.

Officers' Gorget, confirmed 1820.

Drummer. Grenadier Regiments. 1820-1826.

Noncommissioned Officer. Marksmen Platoons of Grenadier Regiments. 1824-1826.

WORK PLAN

Our reprint in based on the original 19th century volumes, to be precise the volumes from 7 to 9 are dedicated to the reign of Paul I; this first part is distributed on 7 volumes, having a numbering from 1 to 7. From number 10 to 18 of the original volumes, the second part is dedicated to the Russian troops under Alexander I. These still being worked on and they will be soon ready, distributed on twenty volumes approximately. Our new edition, the first ever published in English, both on paper and digital format, boasts a large number of color plates, many of them unpublished and coloured by our team of expert artists and scholars of uniformology. Each volume is based on 50/70 plates, always accompanied by the original translated text which describes the uniforms, the organization and the armament of the Russian army of the period.

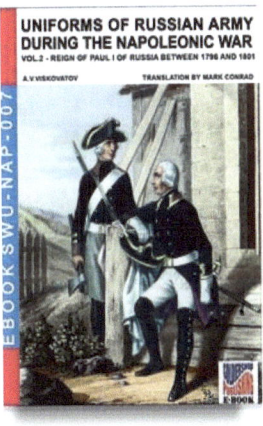

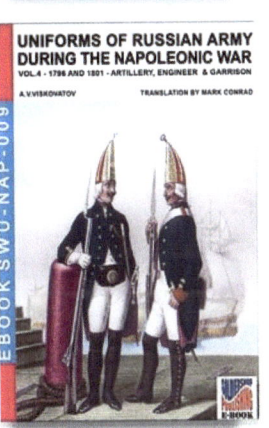